DEAR WHITE WOMAN
DEAR BLACK WOMAN

DEAR WHITE WOMAN DEAR BLACK WOMAN

A Tapestry of Letters for Hope & Healing

Bonita T. Hampton Smith

Published by Ripples Media
www.ripples.media

Copyright © 2025 by Bonita T. Hampton Smith

All rights reserved. No part of this book may be reproduced or used in any manner without written permission of the copyright owner except for the use of quotations in a book review. For more information: publishing@ripples.media

First printing 2025

Cover designed by Burtch Hunter
Typesetting by Carolyn Asman

ISBN 979-8-9918986-0-7 Paperback
ISBN 979-8-9918986-1-4 Hardback
ISBN 979-8-9918986-2-1 E-book

CONTENTS

FOREWORD 13

INTRODUCTION 17
From the Author: Bonita T. Hampton Smith

THE LETTERS 23

Rising With Responsibility 25
Vonnetta

Pulling Back the Veil 29
Angela

When Everyone is Listening 32
Monique

To Change a Culture 37
Jenn

An Invitation to Change 42
Camilla

Yearning for Love and Connection 48
Sabine

Make Space for Her 51
Chantel

A Mutual Love 55
Jenn

Finding My Strength and Voice 59
Ora

Strength of Identity 62
C.Q.

Children Who All Serve the Same God 65
T.B.J.

I Thought Our Struggles Were the Same 69
Margaret

Doing Good Without Fear 73
Anonymous

Breaking Generational Complacency 76
Clare

Claiming Our Space as Women 80
Koddi

Seeing & Celebrating Our Differences 84
Kristin

Finally Exhaling 88
Chantelle

Getting Under Our Skin 92
Dorri

A Concerned Black Mother 97
Aimedra

Turning the Page 100
Kacie

Pulling ScalesOff Your Eyes 104
Antoinette

Linking Arms as Your Sister 107
Kathy

Black Women Dream of Being Mothers Too 111
Julianne

Facing this World Together 116
Tamara

Believe Our Truth 120
Ekaette

Fly in the Buttermilk 123
Betsy

Duality of Similarity 127
Jamine

Moving Past My Assumptions **130**
Maggie

A World Made Just for You **134**
Esther

Seeing Myself as Someone Loveable **138**
Anonymous

Don't Fear My Brother **142**
Jacqueline

Unworthy **145**
Abby

To White Women in Corporate America **148**
Anonymous

Moving Beyond Apologies **151**
Stacy

Sis **155**
Anonymous

Head of the Table **158**
Ashley

Deserving Respect **163**
Lori

Lighting the Way **166**
Anonymous

Picking and Choosing **170**
Anonymous

Forging a Key **174**
Anonymous

Living in Unspoken Segregation **178**
T. M.

Finding My Place in the Solution **183**
Rachel

No Matter What **186**
Anonymous

When Action Causes More Harm than Good 189
Barbara

Seeing Me in this Fight 192
Anonymous

The Multicolor Communal Table 197
Sabine

An Abundance of Allyship 203
Althea

A Student in Search of Truth 207
Gail

It's Time to Get Uncomfortable 210
Attallah

Fueled by Love 213
Carrie

Celebrating Without Apology 215
Sheila

White Woman's Tears 220
Lisa

Heal the Suffering 225
Audrey

Doing the Work 229
Heather

What Allyship Demands 233
Taylor

A Commitment 237
Gina

AFTERWORD 243

ACKNOWLEDGMENTS 249

ABOUT THE AUTHOR & CONTRIBUTORS 253

REFLECTION & DISCUSSION 261

FOREWORD

Historically, Black women have been compelled to navigate the intersections of race, gender, and class to survive in a hostile society. Conversely, White women have faced different struggles, often not contending with the intersection of race and class. During the Civil Rights Movement, Black women fought for equal rights for their men, while White women fought for their own civil rights.

Through *Dear White Woman, Dear Black Woman*, Bonita Hampton Smith starts an incredibly powerful dialogue that has the power to lead to healing race relations among Black and White women.

The truth is, that women of all backgrounds share more commonalities than they realize. This timely work encourages women to confront their shared humanity and, perhaps for the first time, engage in courageous conversations about healing from the fractures caused by "Othering" in our society. Despite racial or ethnic identities, qualifications, experiences, and accomplishments, women are still often viewed as the weaker sex by a dominant male-centric society. This book serves as a crucial step towards recognizing and addressing these issues, fostering understanding, and promoting unity among women.

Dear White Woman, Dear Black Woman has the potential to transform the lives of both the women who participated in this important project and those who read and digest the book.

We have mistakenly believed that Black women and White women are adversaries. This book offers White and Black women the opportunity to empathize with each other's pain and strive for a deeper understanding.

From a psychological perspective, it is imperative for women to heal from a history of oppression and discrimination. Failure to do so can have detrimental effects on their mental, physical, spiritual, and social health. The stress of being a woman in America—earning less than male counterparts for the same positions, fighting for autonomy over their own bodies, facing life-threatening risks during miscarriages, and often feeling voiceless—has become increasingly difficult to manage. This stress is compounded for Black women, who may report to or be supervised by White women unaware of their lived experiences in America, despite the commonalities they share. It is heartening to see that the White women who participated in this project courageously confronted "White Fragility" and spoke their truths with honesty and transparency. The sincerity and truth emanating from the pages of this book are akin to healing waters, cleansing us of impurities—precisely what is needed in this significant season.

Through the letters contained in *Dear White Woman, Dear Black Woman*, women worldwide may begin to experience the truth that has historically been denied to them. It is this truth that has the power to set us all free.

Finally, *Dear White Woman, Dear Black Woman* is an essential read for men. It is imperative for men to recognize that their pursuit of power and control has frequently resulted in unsafe and unhealthy environments for women. This impact extends not only to the women they love but also to the daughters

FOREWORD

they raise. For the survival and progress of our nation, the healing of both White and Black women is crucial. *Dear White Woman, Dear Black Woman* serves as a valuable starting point for this important work.

Gloria Morrow, Ph.D
Licensed Clinical Psychologist

INTRODUCTION

―

From the Author: Bonita T. Hampton Smith

It was not an ordinary day; in fact, we hadn't seen an ordinary day since the World Health Organization declared COVID-19 a global pandemic. The year was 2020, and we were still sheltering in place, grappling with the pandemic, when our lives were interrupted by a video recorded by seventeen-year-old Darnella Frazier, capturing the brutal killing of George Floyd. I will never forget what I witnessed on that day, Monday, May 25, 2020. In my lifetime, I had only seen one individual take their last breath, and that individual was my father.

For my father's death, while I was not prepared, we knew it was inevitable. My father spent the last months of his life in the hospital, where I was privileged to spend the last thirty days of his life by his bedside. During that time, we had many conversations, in one of which my father acknowledged that he was tired and ready to go home. He also shared that his children would fulfill his assignment and that his light would live through me. I was grateful for my father's words and found comfort in a dream I had of him dancing in a big white house.

On November 9, 1991, I retired for the evening, said a prayer to God, and released him from my soul. The following morning, when I entered my father's room, I knew eternity was only moments away for him. I was with my father during his final hour when he transitioned from reality to eternity. I still remember the sound of the electrocardiogram flatlining, signifying there was no electrical activity in my father's heart. Although he was only forty-nine when he passed, he struggled with that heart for the last few years of his life. On November 10, 1991, the beats finally stopped, and my father took his last breath. I screamed.

Beside me stood the Chaplain, who watched in silence and somehow knew I would need the arms he made readily available to catch me as I slowly collapsed. I don't remember his name; I only remember him as an older White gentleman, and his quietness and stillness gave comfort to my soul. I found solace in the arms of a stranger. Before George Floyd, this was the first and only time I had seen someone take their final breath. It was the only death I had ever witnessed.

His death – George Floyd's death was a day when time stood still and then resumed with a vengeance, each second, a stark reminder of a nation whose soul was stained and in desperate need of healing. For an agonizing nine minutes and twenty-nine seconds, a police officer knelt on George Floyd's neck while he was handcuffed and lying face-down on the street. In utter disbelief, we watched a Black man get brutally murdered on television.

Because we were sheltering in place, George's desperate plea for life echoed virtually around the world. With our eyes glued to our televisions, phones, and computers, we watched as George struggled to simply breathe. Over twenty times, we heard a Black man cry, "I can't breathe." Bystanders watched just feet away from George, and I watched, 980 miles away, in my living room.

INTRODUCTION

This was the second time I witnessed someone take their last breath. It was the first brutal killing I witnessed that wasn't a scene from a movie. For George, I didn't scream and there were no arms to console me, only relentless tears that turned into anger. For days, I found myself grappling with what I witnessed. And while I didn't know George, his death left a profound impact on my life. I found myself asking *what do we do with this?* All over the world, we witnessed waves of protests and a pseudo-awakening. I say pseudo because it was incomplete – how could we truly awaken without fully confronting the traumas and pains of our past? How does a nation that doesn't want to deal with its past heal from it?

Like most people during the pandemic, my husband and I found ourselves doing many home projects. One project was expanding our patio, which became my morning place of meditation and solitude. I finally found my *solace* on that patio. The patio is where I would commune with God and sip my morning coffee, which I do in remembrance of my mom. She always loved a good cup of coffee. Each morning she would drink her coffee, read her bible, and talk with God. Sometimes when I am sipping coffee, meditating, and communing with God, I can feel my mom. I know she is somewhere watching over me.

My morning meditations are very intentional. During this period, I often found myself reflecting on our collective wounds and the deep-seated traumas and systemic injustices that have shaped our society. I grappled with anger, frustrated that we seemed eager to move beyond our past without fully acknowledging the profound legacy of slavery, segregation, and ongoing racial discrimination that has left indelible scars on the American psyche. I questioned how to address the foundation of division and mistrust that continues to influence our culture.

There were days when I simply embraced my anger, but I knew I couldn't stay there. My soul needed healing. I needed to release and allow love to be the preeminent force in my life. This quest to embrace, experience, and embody love became my daily intention. As my soul sought to understand my responsibility in our pathway forward, Mrs. Coretta Scott King's words echoed in my soul:

Women, if the soul of a nation is to be saved, I believe that you must become its soul.

As a nation, the tension between Black and White people had reached an all-time high post-George Floyd. We were all trying to figure out what to do. Then it happened, in my place of *solace* – on one of those "not-an-ordinary" days, the inspiration for this book emerged like an electrical current flooding my being. The assignment was clear: invite White women to write letters to Black women, and Black women to write letters to White women. Through these letters, we would begin the birthing and bringing forth healing for a nation grappling with its trauma.

When this vision was given to me, I knew it was not mine alone. I shared this project with four remarkable women – Jenn Graham, Vonnetta West, Monique Richon, and Angela Oxford – and invited them to join me on this journey. Without hesitation, they joined me, and together, we reached out to women across the country, inviting them to share their letters and their hearts. With a commitment to hope and healing, we encountered some fear, unanswered calls, texts, emails, and a few no's. Yet, we found courageous women from all walks of life who said yes to our invitation to share their stories of pain, forgiveness, hope, trauma, healing, and love.

INTRODUCTION

This book, *Dear White Woman, Dear Black Woman: A Tapestry of Letters for Hope and Healing*, is a collection of heartfelt letters compiled to spark a broader dialogue, bringing hope and fostering deep healing. As women, we have the power to change the trajectory of our nation and world.

Together, let's leave a legacy of love, forgiveness, and reconciliation for our children. We do not have to see another life taken away to become the best version and highest expression of humanity. As women, we can change the very soil of this nation and create a world where all of God's children are honored, valued, and loved.

May you discover the threads of connectivity in each letter, linking you to the heart of the composer. May you find your place of solace and be inspired to join us on this journey of hope and healing. Let each letter remind you of our shared humanity and the power of compassion.

Dear White Woman ... Dear Black Woman ...

This is our divine tapestry – each of us a thread of masterfully woven experiences; a testament to the resilience and beauty of what's possible when women forgive, heal and honor each other.

THE LETTERS

Statement of Intent

This collection of letters represents the heartfelt and personal experiences of both White and Black women, each sharing their unique perspectives and lived realities. These letters have been left in their unique form without editing or curation, to serve as a collective reflection and create space for understanding, empathy, and connection.

Our intention is not to speak for anyone, but to invite readers into the individual journeys and reflections of these women, exploring the complexities of identity, race, and personal experience. Each letter is a window into a specific life and viewpoint, offered in the hope of fostering dialogue, compassion, and greater awareness.

We approached this collection with humility and deep respect, understanding that these letters are part of a broader, ongoing conversation about race, gender, and humanity. We encourage you to read with an open mind and an open heart, embracing the diversity of voices and the wisdom they offer.

RISING WITH RESPONSIBILITY
―
Vonnetta

Dear White Woman,

I believe that we can learn to live together well. We have the capacity to understand each other, to be for each other, and to plan a path forward together. Why haven't we done it yet?

I think that there are a few reasons:

1. We have confused guilt with responsibility.

I have never wanted White women to feel guilty for history or to be rendered stagnant because of the burden of the destruction caused by White supremacy across the globe. However, I do earnestly hope that we will one day grasp the power of responsibility. Even if a White woman is not racist in measurable, seen actions, the current condition of humanity, with much of the injustice being the result of a hierarchy of White supremacy, beckons White women to demonstrate a sense of responsibility for moving humanity forward.

I am a Black woman whose ancestors arrived on the shores of this nation in chains and picked cotton in the sweltering Southern sun, and I often feel crushed by the responsibility of the freedom struggle. It is painful and frustrating to witness the shrug of irresponsibility from many White women who either refuse to help humanity eradicate racism or are unapologetically complicit in cultivating oppressive policies, systems, and practices. We are all the ones we have been waiting for. We can rise with responsibility.

2. We do not realize who we are.

As I wrote in the beginning, we have the capacity to understand each other and to plan a path forward together. I believe that the impasse humanity has reached, inclusive of the collective impasse between White women and Black women, reflects our blindness to the Light we were created by and for. We're just living so far below our divine ability to love and to be loved. That is more than regrettable. I believe that it is an abomination and a fundamental blight against humanity.

I imagine and seek the day when there is a multitude of Black women, White women, and women from all races and backgrounds who have built a table together and are charting a course for how we will honor each other. And developing a strategy for how we will work together to rid this world of injustice, including racism and the inhumane hierarchy that prioritizes White women in the workplace, in media, and in other social constructs. We can do that when we know who we are, individually and collectively. We are here to carry light and to liberate with love. We can rise with that realization.

RISING WITH RESPONSIBILITY

We can rise with responsibility.
We can rise with the realization of who we are.
We can rise together to create a global community infused with love, instead of hate, and with light, instead of darkness.

I remain hopeful.

I believe that we can learn to live together well.

Grace and peace,
Vonnetta

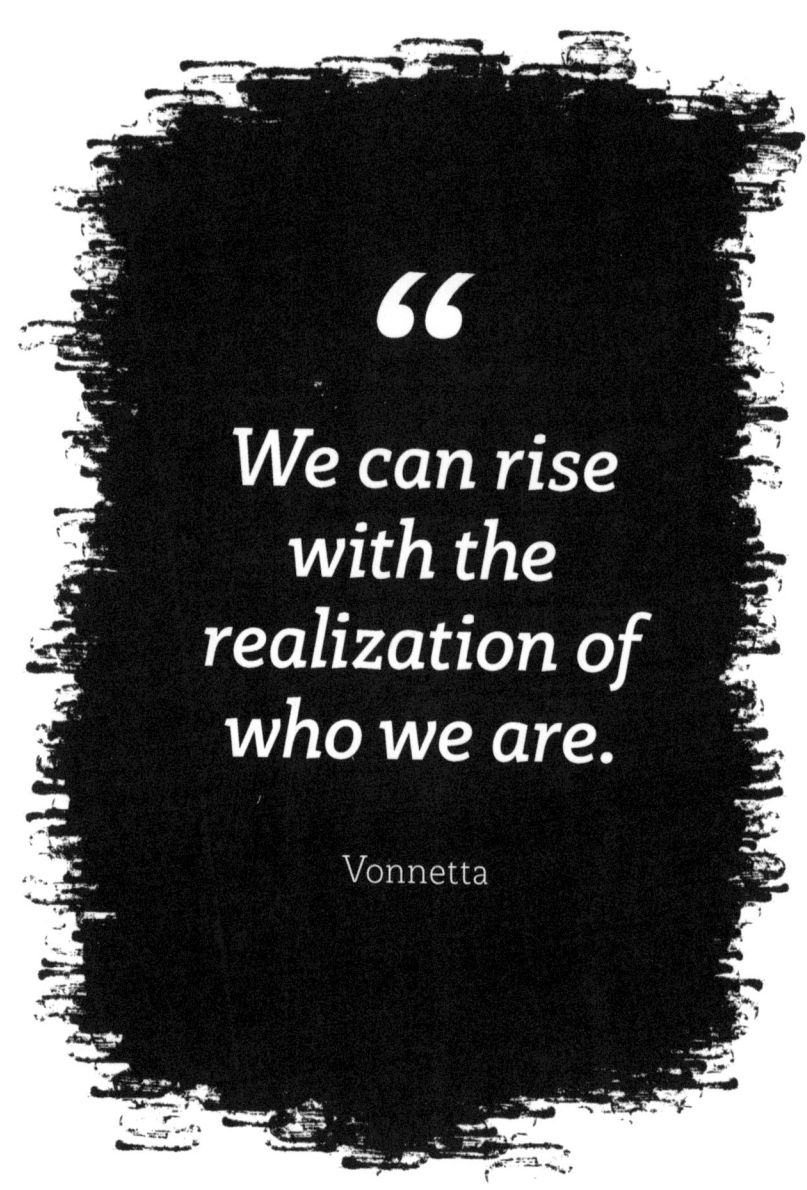

> We can rise with the realization of who we are.
>
> Vonnetta

PULLING BACK THE VEIL
Angela

Dear Black Woman,

Where do I even begin? I wanted to write this letter to say *thank you* – thank you for being my teacher, mentor, and sounding board. You helped me learn and you were kind to me when I was clumsy and clueless and blind to my own ignorance about the systemic oppression that you and your family face every day. But while my heart is full of gratitude for you and your friendship, it is full of shame and regret, seeking forgiveness for placing on you the burden of being my teacher.

You have been patient and gentle with me when I have been so steeped in the privilege that I live in every day that I was lulled into a comfortable state of belief that everyone had the same opportunities if they tried hard enough. You allowed me to see your pain after you arrived at work, having encountered an angry driver who called you the n-word. You were hurt, angry and I was stunned, unsure of how to respond. You allowed me in your home, and we shared meals, and you allowed me to hear your stories – your experience of being followed in stores and of being asked for identification when white friends were not.

DEAR WHITE WOMAN, DEAR BLACK WOMAN

A day that stands out in my mind is when I asked you to tell me what I did not understand about racism and you gently said, "No, you're not ready." I remember the sting of not understanding what that meant. "I'm not ready?" I kept searching and attempting to understand. I was in one of those moments when I realized I did not know what I did not know.

Your words echoed and have hung with me, as time has moved forward. We are far apart now but keep in touch. But today, as I raise my own children of color, the veil of what I was not ready to know has been pulled back. Today I see more clearly that my White culture is so cemented into everyday life that I realize you were required to understand my white world while managing the oppression and systemic racism that White supremacy inflicts on you.

Forgive me for placing the continued burden of making me more comfortable and unscathed while learning about the experience my culture inflicts on you. Know that I know more of what I did not know, it is clearer, and I am more aware. I have a pickaxe and I am here, chipping away at the cemented foundation of White supremacy that has given me a steadied life and racked a burden around yours.

Always grateful,
Angela

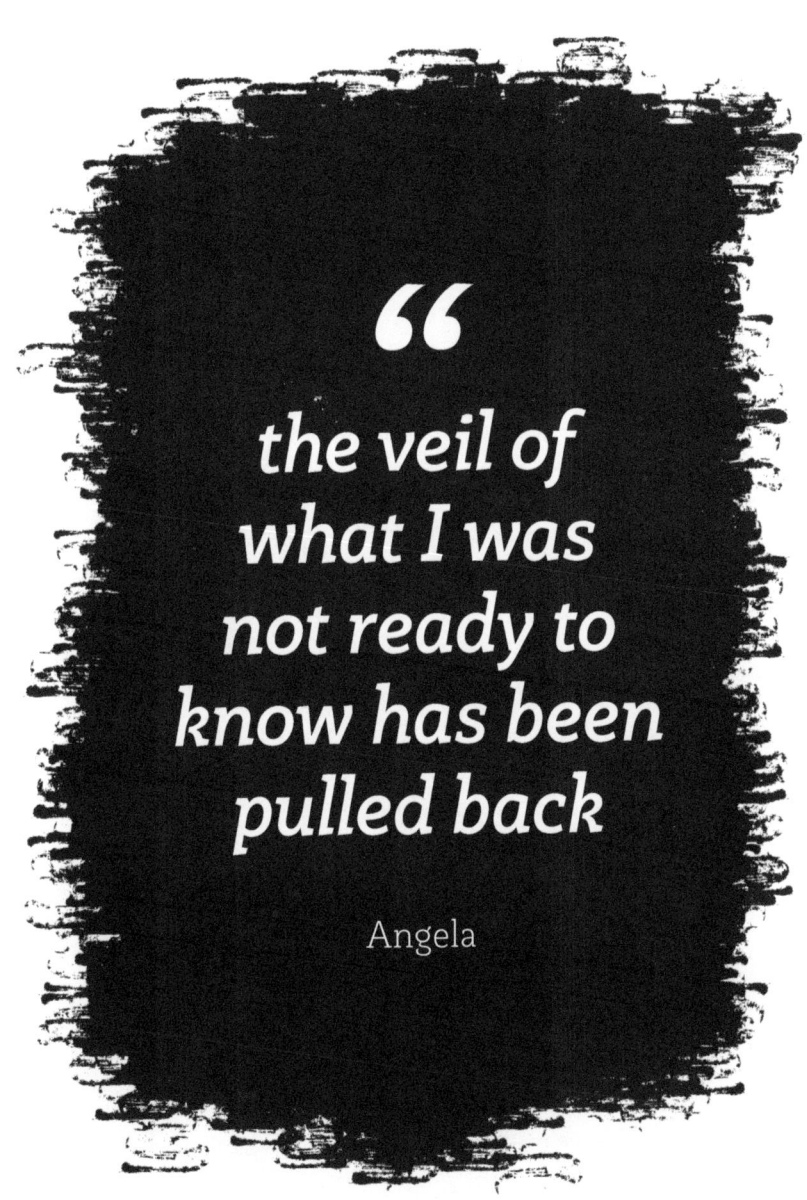

> "the veil of what I was not ready to know has been pulled back
>
> Angela

WHEN EVERYONE IS LISTENING

Monique

"We divest through our commitment to and engagement with anti-racist struggle. Even though that commitment was first made in the mind and heart, it is realized by concrete action, by anti-racist living and being."
–bell hooks, *Killing Rage: Ending Racism*[1]

Dear White Woman,

I have borne witness to your profound ability to remove yourselves from the gross injustices that systemic racism inflicted on Black women in this country. I do not have the privilege to erase the aggressions that I experience in every facet of my life – from running errands at a grocery store, to my workplace environment, to the ivory tower that is the higher education system. Black women are constantly reminded that we are indeed working harder and longer than you and often being paid less. We, Black women, are mentoring Black youth within our reach, and we are eagerly pouring back into the communities that bring us wellness, all while trying to preserve our own hearts, love on our dear ones, and live full, joyful lives.

This is a letter of releasing truth into the universe because for too long, I have whispered words and tucked them away into journals stacked at my bedside. I feel most inclined to shed light on my graduate school experience because it was challenging for different reasons, but mostly because every moment I was working in an in-between space where people were telling me my opinions mattered and at the same time, they weren't listening to a single word.

You see, for me, being a Black woman means living in what W.E.B. Du Bois[2] coined as "double consciousness" where I would advocate for myself and actively seek out support by asking for what I needed – and still be shut out of the world around me. In other words, I was physically present, however the ideas that were most valuable to me couldn't also exist in these post-secondary education spaces. These experiences are a conglomerate of racialized oppression and a sure way to gaslight Black women.

Black women are always praised for our resilience, and it is deeply maddening that the term resilience is thrown around by White women as a badge of honor that you get when you've made it to the other side of enduring consistent challenges. The uphill climb doesn't stop for Black women. You see, to be a Black woman means to endure and endure every moment of every day. To that, I say, no more! We must actively and intentionally rest. Instead of telling me I am resilient, what would be most useful for you and all of the White women reading this would be for you to lift a finger, raise your voice, pay a Black woman, demand accountability, denounce racism and White supremacy and social injustice at every moment in which you encounter them. It is in this way that living and being anti-racist can be actualized in the way that so many Black women envision for a lifetime outside of our own.

DEAR WHITE WOMAN, DEAR BLACK WOMAN

As the child of parents who grew up in the Jim Crow South, as a Black woman in America, as a descendant of slaves, and as an educator who is interested in decency and justice, the fact that White women have come to reckon with themselves all because of the national outcry around police brutality and continued state-sanctioned violence invokes a physical tension in my thirty-three-year-old body. It feels like an unwelcome weighted tightness, it feels like coming up for air after holding my breath for minutes underwater. The idea that it never dawned on you until now that my lived experiences are vastly different from your own is the center of your privilege and a very good place for you to start in your work. Furthermore, what has been so striking for me to witness is that I relied so greatly on Black women to submit letters to this project. This in itself demonstrates your lack of participation around interrogating your beliefs and reflecting upon how you continuously inflict violence on the Black women who you call friends, colleagues and/or family. Black women have historically been doing the work of promoting racial justice and education equity while simultaneously working to heal ourselves. Every day we break through the glass ceilings while White women are busy marinating in their proximity to White men.

I want to make it very clear to you that I am not here to repair anything. As a Black woman, I will not uphold the idea that I owe you explanations. Many of my lived experiences exist in the ways they do because you have remained silent in rooms where everyone listened to you. You have lived in a place where complacency and mediocrity are your neighbors. You have lived in a world where your families moved you in the middle of grade school so you could attend predominantly White public schools; a world where you date Black men behind closed doors but would never bring them home to your families. White women, you live in a world where you went out in higher numbers than you did the four years prior to vote for a man who will go down in history as the most unqualified, racist, sexist, and bigoted President of the United States and yet you voted for him again. I am certainly not here to repair but rather to look you in your eyes and let you know that I have always seen you, and you have not been a safe place – nor a place where I can trust that my values and my life matter to you – on the ballots you submit at the polls, at the dinner tables to break bread, at or in the cubicles parallel to my own.

In this moment and in every moment to come, you need to get your people and do your work. That is the way forward from here.

In deep reflection and truth,
Monique

[1] hooks, bell . (1995). Killing Rage: Ending Racism. New York: Henry Holt and Company.

[2] Du Bois, W. E. B. (1903) The Souls of Black Folk. New York: Bantam Books.

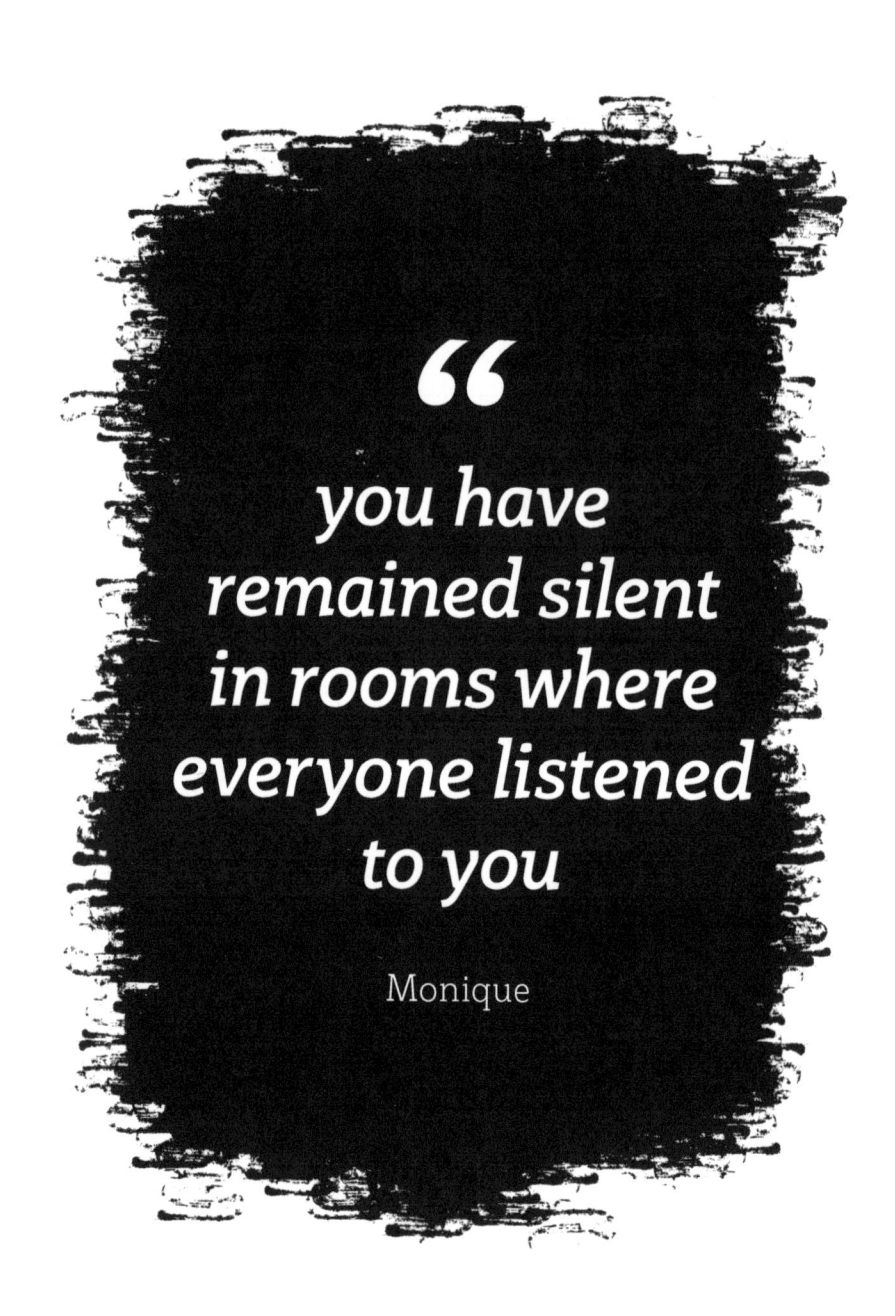

> "you have remained silent in rooms where everyone listened to you

Monique

TO CHANGE A CULTURE

Jenn

Dear Black Woman,

Thank you. Thank you for your love. Thank you for your grace. And thank you for creating space while I ventured on a learning journey, seeking truth and understanding.

The truth is, I will never fully understand what your experience has been like. But I have never been stopped by a cop or questioned if I belong here. I've never wondered if I didn't get the job because of the color of my skin. And I won't fear for my son's death if he is pulled over by a police officer or feel I must have that conversation with him. This is my White privilege.

My journey of understanding started three days after the 2016 election. I attended the Race Forward conference in Atlanta, just a few miles from my home. It was there that I learned a metaphor for racism. It was described in this way, "For so many, people think racism is a shark that you can trap and remove, but really, it's the water. It's the culture in which we live and breathe."

One of the breakout sessions titled "White Saviorism" was so packed that many White women were sitting in the aisles cross-legged, eager to learn how they could play a role. But what we learned was how to get out of the way of Black women. I learned that jumping straight to action could cause more harm than good. And what was needed the most was for White women to confront the truth and origin of racism, and just sit in the discomfort. It was exactly what I needed to hear, and it launched me on my own journey of understanding race.

Soon after, I found myself in Minneapolis, at the YWCA in April of 2017 for a Racial Equity Institute, a two-day workshop focused on the basic principles of racial justice. I sat in a circle surrounded by fifteen other leaders from around the city as we learned about the real history of how America was formed. I learned how "race" is an invented social concept used as a wedge to divide people for power and control dating all the way back to colonial times.

It was at that moment that my lens on the world changed. And I finally began to see.

I saw how every system suffers from systemic racism. I saw how systemic racism had been programmed and maintained into our laws, our policies and our culture. These were systems built by white people, for white people. It's easy to see when you look at systems from housing to education to healthcare, each with enormous disparities known as "the achievement gap," "health disparities," and "income inequality."

I felt like I had learned the real history that wasn't taught in the public school system where I grew up. I even learned how this was intentional, and how Baby Boomers and Gen X children in the South were taught a false version of U.S. history, promoting the idea that the Confederacy's cause in the American Civil War was just and heroic, and not centered on slavery. It went so far as to portray the White South as the victim.

What startled me the most was to learn that this false "Lost Cause" narrative became so prevalent across the South for over a century because a group of White women, the United Daughters of the Confederacy, organized and advocated for the rewrite of the history books in the South! And I wept when I learned that even though black women played a pivotal role in the Women's Suffrage Movement, white women benefited first from the right to vote. You and your sisters had to wait another forty-five years until the Civil Rights Act of 1964 passed to remove the barriers of poll taxes, literacy tests, and violence so that you could simply vote.

I understand why Black women feel betrayed by White women. I would too. I feel a sense of rage when I think about how often White women have failed to stand in solidarity with Black women, whether through inaction, misunderstanding or blatant bigotry.

But my rage does not serve you.

If anything has come to light in this journey, it is that to change a culture, we must change the stories. And I must change my own story first. I must change my mindset from a victim of shame to a powerful agent of influence.

One way I aim to serve you is to use my privilege to bring people together to share stories, express emotions, and bring about healing for ourselves and past generations.

Women are sisters. Women unified with one another are powerful beyond imagination.

As your sister, I hold myself responsible for lifting you up every chance I get. I engage in difficult conversations, and advocate for change in both big and small ways. I see every encounter with you as an opportunity to create space, build connection, and find ways to support you. I commit to wielding my privilege on your behalf, standing in solidarity with you, and calling on my peers.

I know this isn't enough to make up for all that has wronged you for generations. I want you to know that I'm committed to building a more inclusive world and bringing others along with me.

You are not alone. You are so loved. And you are perfect as you are.

Your sister,
Jenn
Atlanta, Georgia

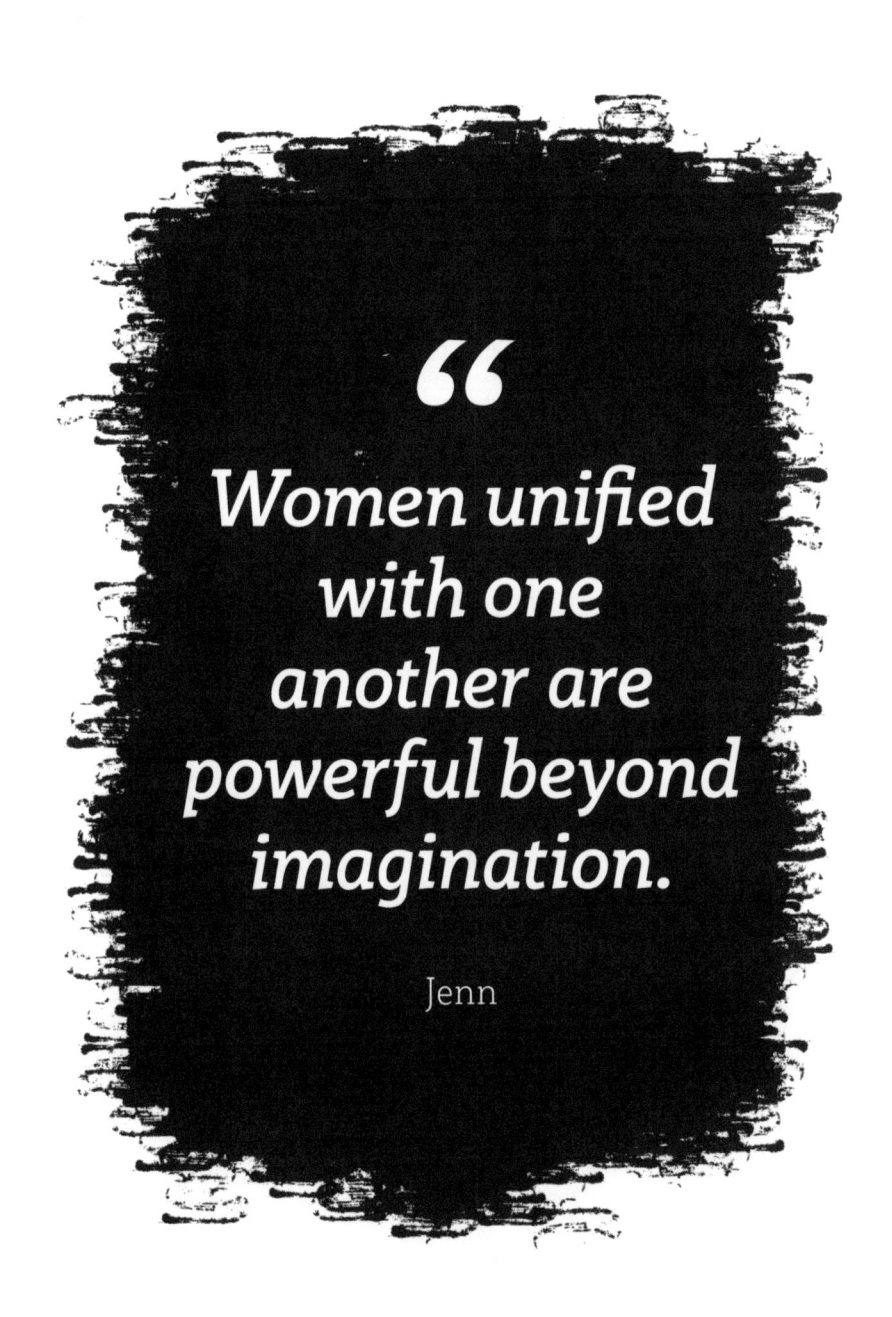

> **Women unified with one another are powerful beyond imagination.**
>
> Jenn

AN INVITATION TO CHANGE

Camilla

Dear White Woman,

I want to share a part of my life with you, a glimpse into the moments that shaped my understanding of race, identity, and justice in America. My story is not unique, but it is personal, and it has defined the way I see our shared world. I hope that through these words, you'll not only hear my experience but feel it.

I grew up with two homes: Tennessee in the winter and upstate New York in the summer. Each place gave me its own lessons about race, but the winters were harsher than the cold itself. In Mount Pleasant, Tennessee, I went to a high school where the unspoken rules of race were loud enough to echo through the hallways. These rules weren't written down, but they were enforced by attitudes, comments, and choices people made about who belonged where.

Our girls basketball team was full of talent, many of us Black girls who poured our hearts into the game. We were celebrated for our skills on the court, cheered on by crowds of parents and classmates. But that acceptance had its limits. You see, our cheerleading squad had a rule that only three Black girls could be on the team at any given time. I still remember the White woman coach telling me this, not as an apology or explanation, but simply as a fact. "This is how it is," she seemed to say. And that moment changed everything for me.

I was fifteen years old when I first fully understood that you could love the way we entertain you, and admire our talent, but still believe we aren't equal. It was a slap in the face – a sharp reminder that there were lines we weren't allowed to cross, limits to how far we could dream or aspire in spaces you controlled. I asked myself, why? Why do you enjoy watching us perform, but not believe we can be equal to you? Why is it that even the ones who have so little still see themselves as superior to us?

That question never left me, and as I grew older, I started to understand that this wasn't just about cheerleading squads or basketball games. It was about a system that was designed to limit us, to tell us in a thousand subtle and blatant ways that we were "less than."

In Tennessee, I saw how the school system was built to filter Black and brown children toward failure. By the third grade, they were already deciding which of us would be funneled into the prison pipeline, which of us would be forgotten by the system. Studies have shown that by the time Black children reach the third grade, educators begin to make predictions about their future academic and behavioral success based on stereotypes, often leading to harsher disciplinary actions for Black students compared to their white peers (Wald & Losen, 2003). The same system only acknowledges Black history once a year – February, the shortest month. And you, White Woman, stood by and allowed it to happen. Some of you may not have actively participated, but silence is a powerful weapon, and it keeps this system running just the same.

Why are we not fighting together to teach All-American history? Why are Black contributions to this nation treated as footnotes instead of integral chapters? Why do you remain quiet when the system continues to harm my people when you have the privilege of your voice being heard?

Growing up, I learned that for people who look like me, the battle against racism is ongoing and unrelenting. We fight it in the streets, in the classroom, in our workplaces, and even in our own minds. I learned that faith and resilience could carry me far, but not far enough to break the chains you still hold. My faith taught me that we are all created in the image of God, but your actions often contradicted that teaching. How can you claim to share that belief and yet refuse to see me as your equal?

You may be wondering why I'm sharing all this with you. Why a letter addressed to *Dear White Woman*? It's because I want you to know what it feels like to carry this history, this weight. I want you to understand what it's like to walk into a room and know that, for some people, the color of your skin is all they need to know about you. But more than that, I want you to realize the power you hold to change things.

I'm not writing to accuse you but to invite you – to invite you to listen, to reflect, and to act. You have the privilege to remain untouched by the injustices that affect my community, but you also have the privilege to help dismantle them. The political divide, the systemic racism, the inequality – they persist because too often, people like you don't see them as your fight. But this isn't just about Black people. This is about what kind of country we want to live in, and what kind of future we want for our children.

We live in a country where the divide between us isn't just political, it's historical. It's ingrained in our laws, our policies, and our culture. We live in a country where Black people are three times more likely to be killed by the police than White people (Mapping Police Violence, 2023). We live in a country where White privilege, a system of advantages based on race, allows you to navigate through life without the same barriers that I face daily. White privilege doesn't mean your life isn't hard – it means that your skin color isn't one of the things making it harder (McIntosh, 1989).

What do I hope you take away from this? That our stories matter, that our pain is real, and that your silence or inaction only perpetuates the problems. I hope you understand that while our experiences may differ, we share a common humanity. And with that humanity comes a responsibility – yours and mine – to fight for a world where all of us are truly equal.

This isn't easy, and it won't happen overnight. But if we are to heal as a nation, we must start by acknowledging the deep wounds of our past and present. And that begins with honest, heartfelt dialogue. White women like you have the ability to use your privilege to amplify the voices of Black women, to stand alongside us in the fight for justice and equality. We need you to be more than allies – we need you to be co-conspirators in the work of dismantling racism.

It was an honor to be invited to participate in this project. Writing this letter to you has been an invaluable experience, allowing me to express the pain and frustration, but also the hope that we can create a better future. I pray that as you read this, you do so with an open heart and a willingness to not only hear, but to act.

Sincerely,
Camilla, a Black Woman Who Believes in Change
Doctorate of Theology

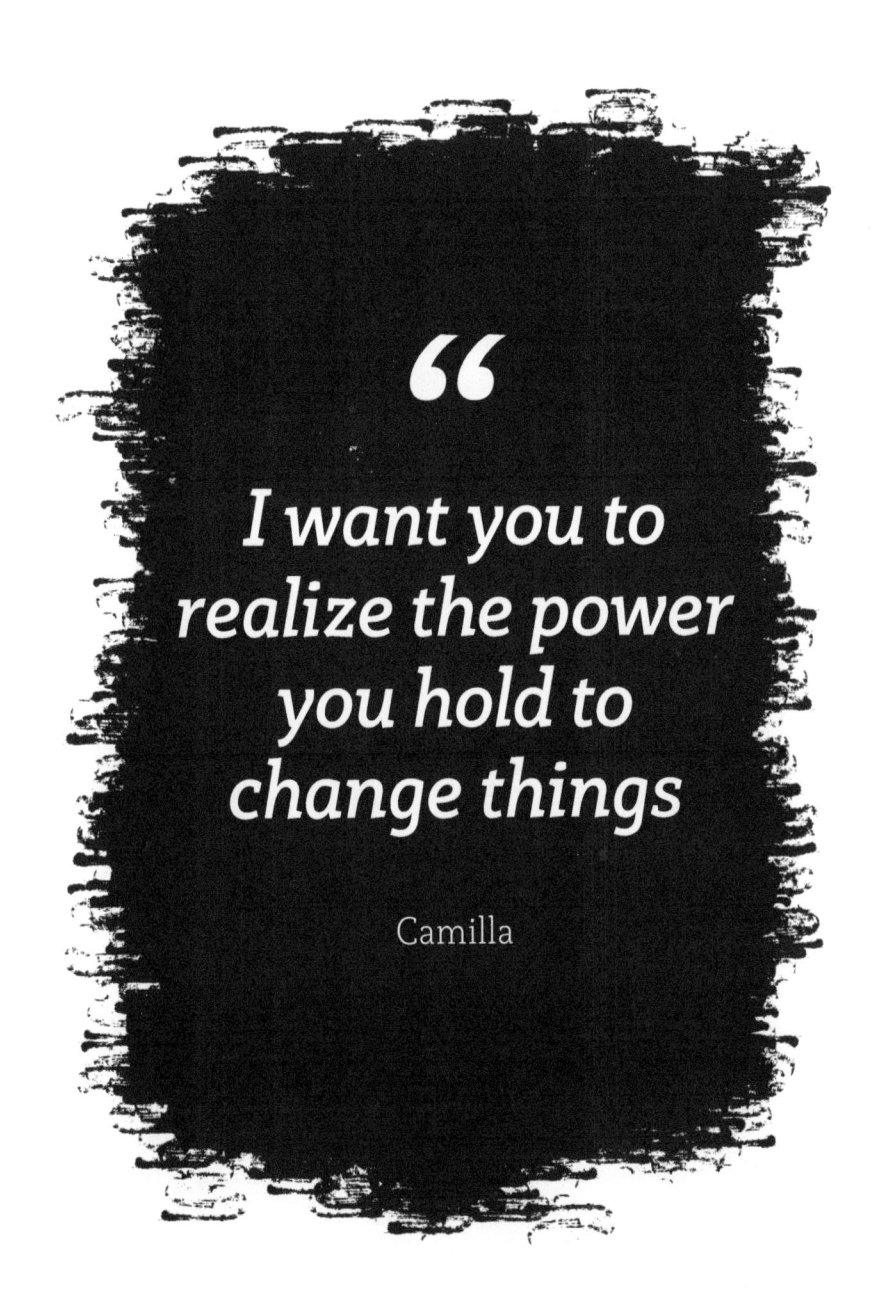

> *I want you to realize the power you hold to change things*
>
> Camilla

YEARNING FOR LOVE AND CONNECTION
—
Sabine

Dear Black Woman,

I am drawn to you and your uniqueness. I admire your beauty, strength, and powerful energy. I value your friendship because that human experience feels good. Is that weird?

I have people asking me if I am gay (I love rainbow everything) or if I have a Black background (due to my hourglass figure or my love for blues/hip hop). I understand that beauty is in the eye of the beholder but I truly don't understand why people hate those with darker skin tones. I find it beautiful. Why are we defined by these external social pictures? It doesn't make sense to me, and I get upset when I see and hear it. It seems to run deep in families and religions.

I am a very curious person, always asking questions that sometimes can upset people as it feels inquisitive. I have always wanted to be part of the change, but I don't always know where to start. I keep it at my local level. You are different. And that is good. Our society and community needs diversity to be better for ourselves and our children. You are showing me that being different is good. I try new things as a fifty-year-old woman in a place where I sometimes don't belong...

Why, do you ask? Well, I moved to the U.S. from France in my teenage years, attending an American high school, trying to fit in. I had limited exposure to American culture, and I had little knowledge of the language and segregated culture here. I didn't understand why the difference in my skin as a freckled girl with an accent was not accepted and even a threat. I went from being a confident "head of my class' kid in Paris, to a quiet high school student searching for my place in society. I was in all the advanced classes, but the social aspect of school was excruciating.

As I write this letter to you, it is even difficult to find the words of how miserable I was as a teen in America. Fortunately, I found a couple of friends who supported me. And with resilience, stubbornness, I decided to thrive in adult life. Today I believe friendships and true conversations are the most important. To be honest, I still don't understand why people separate people into these buckets, but I yearn to learn and support the good and love in humans and children. Finally I am a mom, and I yearn for my daughter to live in a world with love and acceptance for human connections, no matter their physical look.

Sincerely,
Sabine

> *I yearn for my daughter to live in a world with love and acceptance for human connections*
>
> Sabine

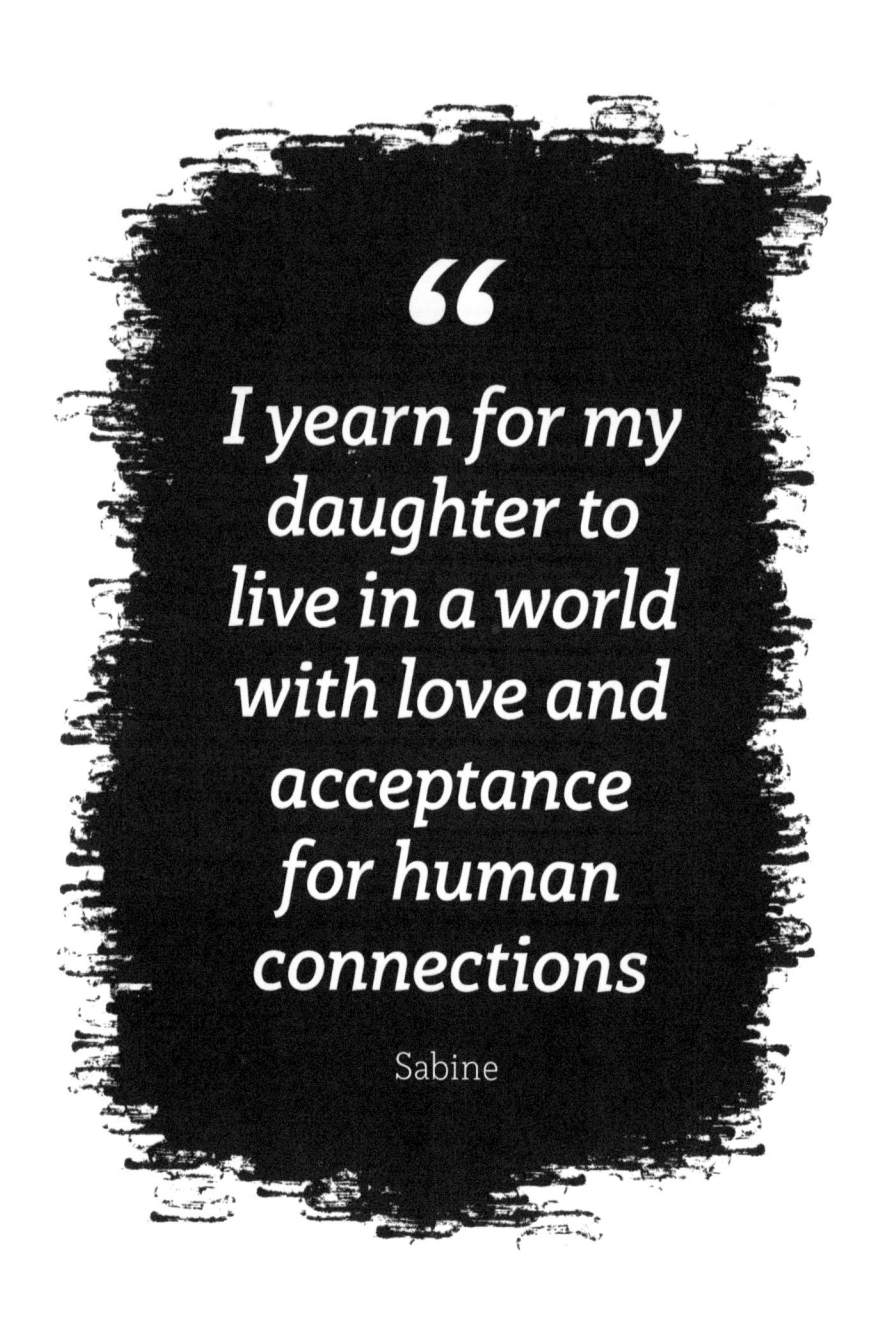

MAKE SPACE FOR HER

Chantel

Dear White Woman,

I want to start this letter by saying that what I'm about to share comes from a place of love and honesty. I believe in us – women – as a collective force, but I also know that if we're really going to move forward together, we need to have some difficult conversations about race, privilege, and allyship. And while these topics can be uncomfortable, they are also the ones that matter most.

As a Black woman, there have been countless times in professional spaces where my opinion wasn't asked for, not because I didn't have something to contribute, but because people didn't even think to ask. They didn't see me. And that can be hard, especially when you know that your perspective, your lived experience, could add so much value to the conversation.

But this letter isn't about pointing fingers. It's about inviting you to recognize the privilege you hold and to think about how you can use that for good. Yes, White women have certain privileges – privileges that come with being part of a system that wasn't built with women like me in mind. But here's the thing: that privilege can also be a powerful tool for change. When you're invited to sit at the table – and I know you've worked hard to get there – you have the opportunity to make sure that someone like me has a seat too.

That's where true allyship comes in. It's about looking around the room and asking yourself, "Whose voices are missing?" It's about sharing the space you've earned and making sure that others are given the same opportunity to be heard.

I know the word "privilege" can be a tough pill to swallow. It can feel like an accusation, but it's not. Privilege doesn't mean you haven't struggled, and it doesn't take away from the work you've done to get to where you are. What it does mean is that there are systems in place that have made your path just a little bit easier in ways that may not always be visible. And that's okay. The real question is, what are you going to do with that knowledge?

I've seen what happens when White women use their privilege to lift others up. I've been in rooms where a woman like you has made space for me, has amplified my voice, and has made sure I was part of the conversation. And let me tell you, those moments are so powerful in changing the way we all show up for each other.

Diversity and inclusion isn't about drawing lines between us, but about tearing down the walls that have kept some of us out for far too long. We, as women, know what it feels like to be underestimated, to be overlooked, to be told that we don't belong. That's where our common ground lies. The struggles aren't always the same, but they come from a shared place of wanting to be seen, heard, and valued.

So, here's what I'm asking of you: know your privilege, but don't stop there. Question the systems that benefit you and consider how you can challenge them for the greater good. When you're sitting at that table, look around. Is there a Black woman there with you? If not, ask why. Make space for her, and when she's there, listen. Ask her opinion, and let her voice be part of the decisions being made. That's how you show up as an ally.

This work isn't easy. It's messy, uncomfortable, and sometimes even painful. But it's also necessary. And the more we engage in these conversations, the more we'll grow. Not just as individuals, but as a community of women who are committed to lifting each other up.

I believe in that future, and I believe in us. Let's be brave enough to have these conversations, and let's make sure no one is left out again.

With love,
Chantel

> *Make space for her, and when she's there, listen.*
>
> Chantel

A MUTUAL LOVE

Jenn

Dear Black Woman,

When I leaned into the healing still needed for Black and White women to feel like true sisters, I got cold feet to send my letter. I became insecure and I asked myself, what could I possibly contribute to help us continue forward in a healing to sisterhood?

I concluded this one, very important, message: *I LOVE YOU*.

Even though this message encapsulates all I want to say, we owe it to each other to exchange about everything and anything. These are hard conversations, but we empower ourselves with the ability to talk to each other. So, here is the my lengthier note to you beyond the short of *I LOVE YOU:*

———

My Beloved Sister,

When I was younger, I believed that rules were meant to be broken. So, I broke them as I pleased. I didn't hold this belief from some elitist idea of myself but from a rebel's perspective. I disliked anything that was "the man" and the system holding me or anyone else down. With age and time, I hope to have gained some perspective on life. With more awareness, my own White privilege is unmistakable. I wonder what would have happened if I was Black instead of White? How has that difference shaped you and me?

I cringe at the thought that I haven't earned my achievements and worse yet that I might have received blessings at the expense of others. However, I acknowledge the ugly truth that despite the hardships I have personally overcome, *I have benefited solely because I am White.* My privilege started long before I was born, but I'm still responsible to make amends by "paying for the sins of my father." I can see the ugly privilege clearly with "Karen." I apologize for her. I cringe at her. She is laughable at best and, at her worst, a weaponization of Whiteness. I wish there were no barriers between people because of skin color; but, I recognize our experiences of life are different because the color of our skin is different.

Writing this letter has helped me to be aware of the need to continue to educate myself more about our different experiences. You may think I'm not motivated to educate myself, or worse yet, that I'm entitled to ask you to do the work, but I'd sincerely appreciate any help you can offer in my continued education and ways that I could start to make amends. I'm inviting you to honestly talk to me and hopefully have some patience that I'm another human being trying my best, miserable sometimes and laughable often, in this effed up and beautiful world.

Participating in this project was not only an opportunity for me to grow personally, but more importantly, a way to communicate my desire to stand with you and for you – to know that you have my support, my ears to listen to what you need, and my actions to help contribute to making change. I stand with you.

Thank you for this opportunity to examine my own choices and thank you for taking your time to read my letter. I look forward to reading your letters. I am grateful to have honest conversations with you dear Black woman.

Love,
Jenn
performer.composer.educator

P.S. I know that cultural appropriation is wrong. Taking something, intellectual or physical, from another for ones own profit and to claim it as ones own is wrong. I'm going to be honest though, the area of cultural appropriation in our relationship leads me to question:

What constitutes cultural appropriation between Black and White women?

When it comes to styling one's self after another's culture, is there any room for the concept of "imitation is the sincerest form of flattery"?

Can one express admiration and celebration by adopting another culture's elements as part of their own? Or, does adopting another's cultural elements as one's own create stereotypes without honoring the deeper meaning behind those beautiful things?

If a person could share in a mutual love of any culture's unique beauty, might we become more unified as humans loving the beauty in each other? Or, do we need to retain our uniqueness?

> *a mutual love of any culture's unique beauty*
>
> Jenn

FINDING MY STRENGTH AND VOICE
—
Ora

Dear White Woman,

I grew up as a Black woman in the South, in a small town called Marianna, Arkansas. From an early age, I knew what it meant to dream big despite humble beginnings. Raised in poverty, I held on to the vision of a better life, a life where I could thrive and succeed. I pursued that vision with unwavering determination, earning not one but five degrees in business and technology, driven by my belief in the American dream – a dream of self-sufficiency, prosperity, and opportunity for all. But along the way, I learned that no matter how hard I worked, no matter how much I accomplished, some doors would always be shut to me because of the color of my skin.

I've witnessed White colleagues advancing in their careers, often not due to any extraordinary talent or expertise, but because of their connections – the people they knew. Time and again, I found myself as the only Black woman – or sometimes the only woman at all – in my professional spaces. This did not make me feel included or welcomed. Instead, it made me feel that I had to work ten times harder just to be seen as equal, just to prove that I belonged. Unlike my peers, I felt I had little room for mistakes. Opportunities for mentorship were few and far between, and I often felt tolerated rather than genuinely valued. This environment chipped away at my confidence, making me reluctant to speak up or assert myself, even when I had something important to contribute.

Growing up in the South, I have seen the painful realities of racism and discrimination firsthand. I learned that my own father, a farm laborer, was taken advantage of by his employer, who exploited his lack of education and business knowledge. His employer filed his taxes and kept the earned income credits meant for our family, disguising them as wages or occasional bonuses. It wasn't until my mother began working that we uncovered this deception, but by then, the damage was done, and the lesson was learned – racism wasn't just something we saw on the news; it was woven into the very fabric of our daily lives.

Today, as a Black woman in my mid-fifties, I have grown into my strength and found my voice. I know my worth and refuse to let anyone define it for me. I am an entrepreneur, business consultant, speaker, and author, and I am grateful for the life I've built. Yet, my journey has taught me that achieving success for myself is not enough. I am committed to mentoring others and helping them find the courage and confidence to pursue their own dreams. I have never asked for a handout – only for a fair chance: a chance to be seen and valued for who I am, to be recognized as a capable, intelligent woman whose worth is not determined by the color of her skin. My wish is for a world where we can all coexist, respect one another, and come together in peace and harmony.

Sincerely,
Ora

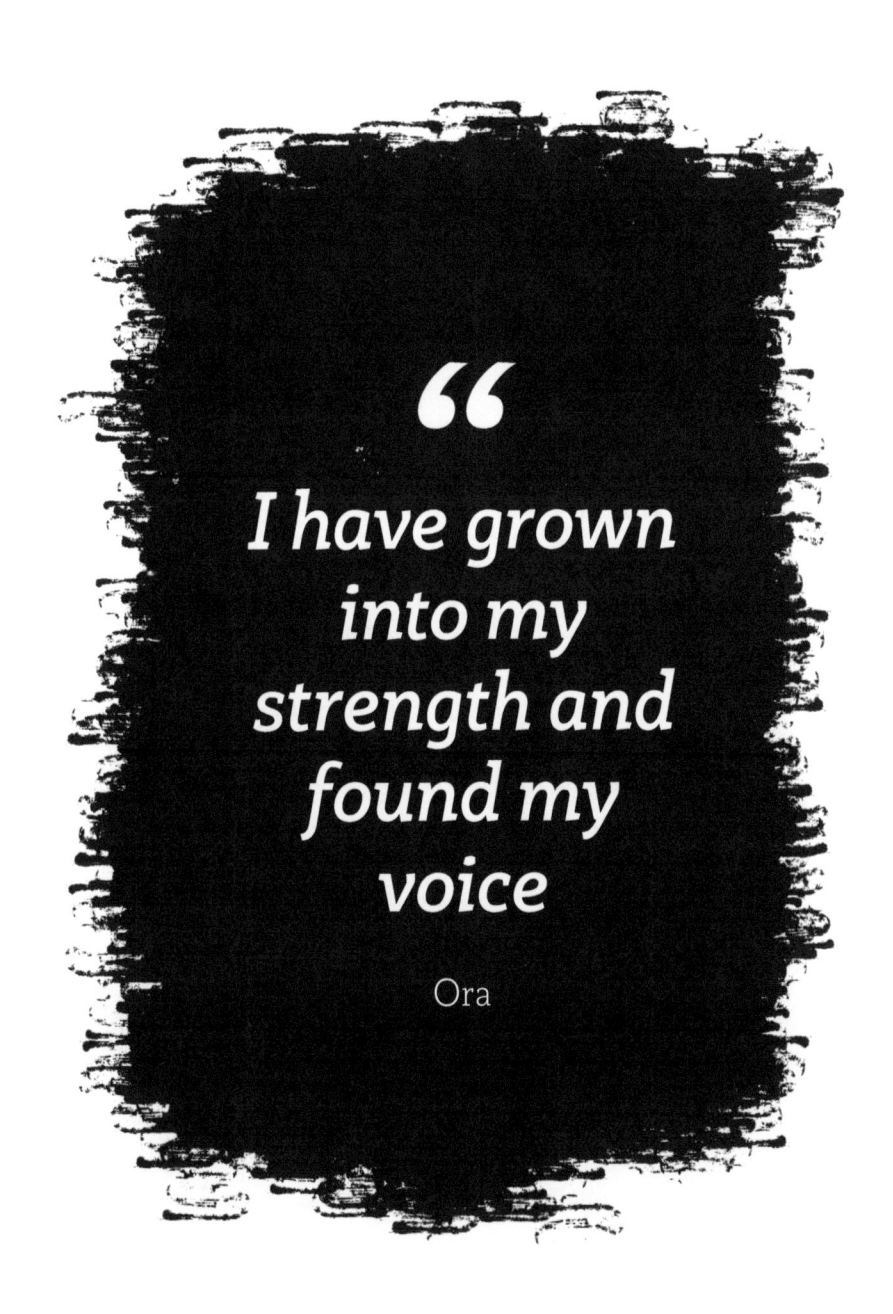

> *I have grown into my strength and found my voice*
>
> Ora

STRENGTH OF IDENTITY

C.Q.

Dear Black Woman,

You are the true unsung heroes in my life, and I am sorry that it has taken me nearly three decades of my existence to acknowledge this fact out in the open. Black women have been integral in becoming who I am today. You have been the teachers throughout various areas of my life. From the Black women who were not given credit throughout history that led to the shaping of today's society, to the Black women who taught me in school, facilitated my religious knowledge, and shaped my identity.

I specifically want to address the Black women of past and present who are Muslim. I hold such deep gratitude and respect for you. I can't imagine the strength it took in the 1950s and 1960s, when Malcolm X and Muhammad Ali were in the spotlight for Black Americans and Black Muslim Americans. Not only were you discriminated against and targeted for being Black and being a woman, but you boldly went forth and converted to Islam as well. You propelled a movement in the background while navigating a patriarchal and deeply racist society.

My first mentor as a new Muslim in 2018 was a Black woman. As a convert herself, she was so passionate about helping other new

STRENGTH OF IDENTITY

Muslims. She was a guiding source in understanding the start of my journey in Islam. To this day, she remains actively involved in the community – I don't think I've ever been to the masjid for prayer without seeing her conversing with the other sisters (and occasionally telling the rest of us to silence our phones and tighten up our gaps in the prayer line). She emphasized in one of our classes for new Muslims that Black people are converting to Islam at a higher rate than other populations in the U.S.[1] I sometimes wonder if I would have converted if Black women were not so instrumental in the Muslim faith growing in popularity in America.

My final note of appreciation and awe is this: I felt immensely vulnerable when I wore a hijab for the first time, not being used to a part of my identity being so prominently on display. But that was a choice for me. And it remains a choice for me every time I leave my home. Whereas your skin and ancestry are with you as closely as your shadow, tied with you from the day you were born. I went from feeling like I blended into the background of my privileged existence to feeling on display. People could now take one look at me and know something about me that feels very sacred. Realizing that even this jarring experience pales in comparison to living day-to-day as a Black woman is humbling.

The strength you have is incredible. The positive impacts I've gained from the Black women in my life feel wholly undeserved. I respect you, I value you, and I want to put the spotlight on how important you have been and still are to me and to society at large. We wouldn't be here without you.

With love,
C.Q.

[1] "Religious Landscape Study." Pew Research Center, May 12, 2015.

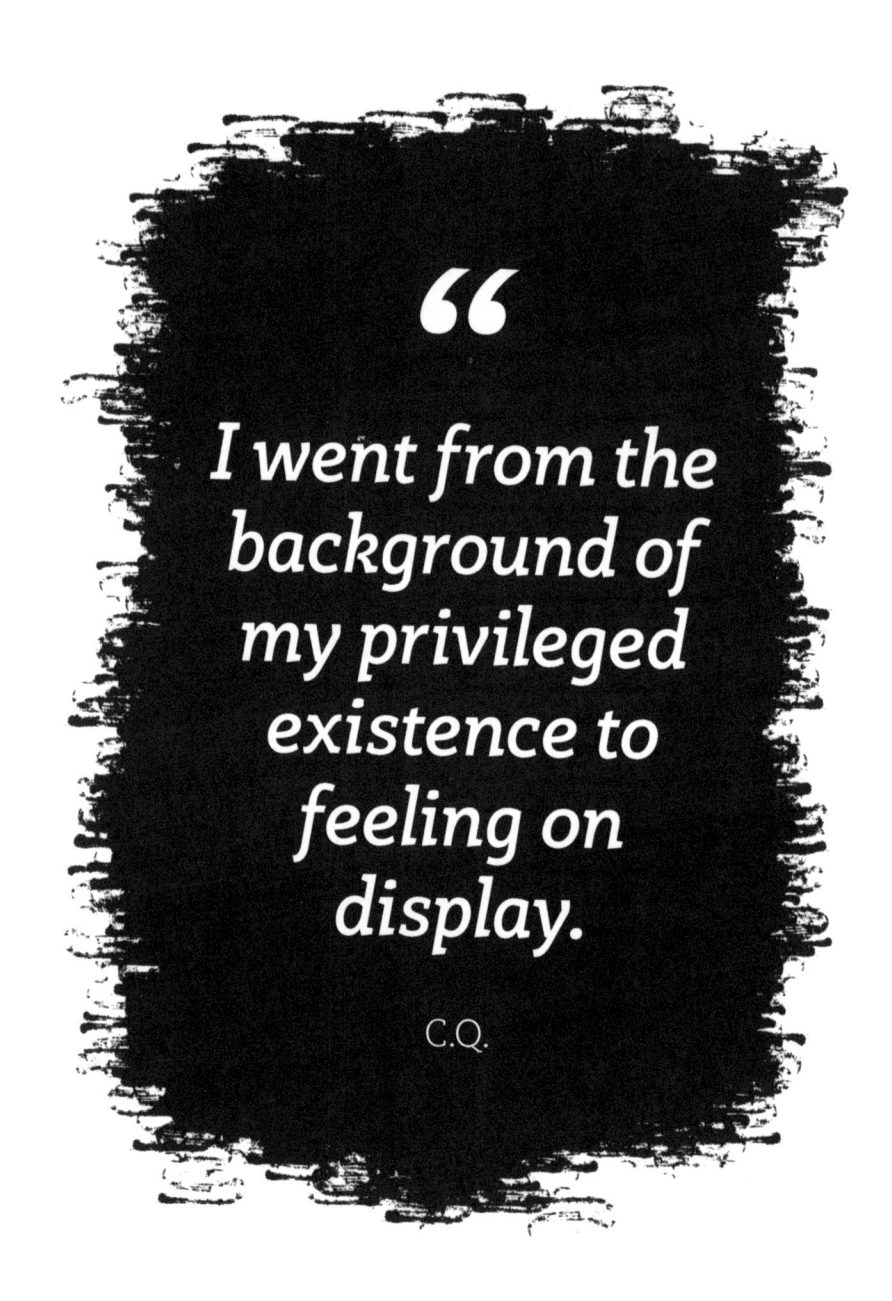

> "I went from the background of my privileged existence to feeling on display.

C.Q.

CHILDREN WHO ALL SERVE THE SAME GOD
―
T.B.J.

Dear White Woman,

I am a Black woman who joined a predominately White United Methodist Church in 2006. I moved to Desoto, Texas, after living in Northern Virginia for ten years. I have always been an active member in the Baptist Church. But, this church was in my neighborhood, it was a small congregation, and we enjoyed the pastor.

We visited the church not knowing that it was a predominately White church. It was a beautiful church, and we wanted to visit. As we entered the church, everyone was so nice and inviting. We were met at the door with hugs and we heard a great sermon from the White pastor. The same Sunday evening, the pastor showed up at our home with a warm loaf of bread. How awesome! This pastor had definitely convinced us to return to his church again. We started attending the church regularly. Again, everyone was really nice. Our Sunday School was great. We were making friends at this church.

However, the United Methodist Church pastors only serve a limited time at one location. I was not used to that in the Baptist Church. In less than a year after we started attending this church, they announced that this White, male pastor was being replaced by a Black, female pastor. Oh my! Little did I know that things were about to change!

I was really excited to learn that a Black, female pastor would be joining this congregation. She was well-known in the community, and I was already impressed with what I had seen on her. Unfortunately, the White congregants did not feel the same way. In less than a month, about 80% of the White members moved!

Dear White woman, why do White women not fight to support Black women in leadership? Especially in the church...

The United Methodist Church is not a stranger to women in leadership/pastors. In fact, many women in ministry move to the United Methodist Church for more opportunities to pastor. This particular church was actually founded by a married couple and they co-pastored for years.

This experience continues to confirm the statement Dr. Martin Luther King, Jr made in 1963 that "It is appalling that the most segregated hour of Christian America is 11 o'clock on Sunday morning."

Why was that still the case in 2006? Why is it still the case now? The flee of White members from this church became personal for me. Why was it OK for us to serve together under the leadership of a White man and not OK under the leadership of a Black woman? White women, why would you allow your children to see blatant racism in the church? Did it matter to you that we had to explain this to our children?

My hope is that women would start supporting other women, especially in the faith community. We might deliver our message a little bit differently, but, we are saying the same thing. We might speak with authority, but, we are passionate and want you to feel that same passion. Our goal should be to embrace similarities, not look for differences. We are all God's children and we all serve the same God. Let's do it together!

Sincerely,
T.B.J.
Desoto, Texas

> "We are all God's children and we all serve the same God

T.B.J.

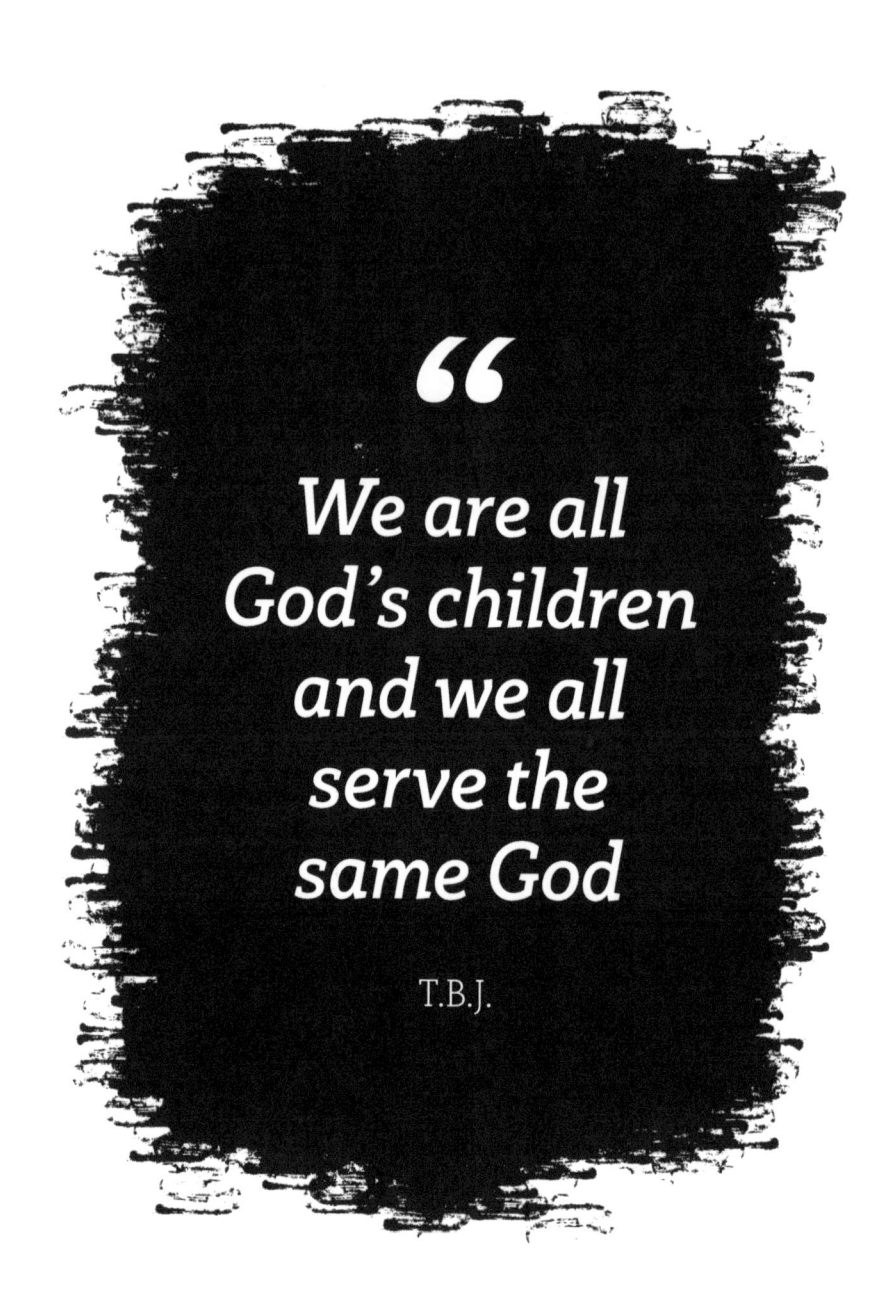

I THOUGHT OUR STRUGGLES WERE THE SAME

Margaret

Dear Black Woman,

I'm ashamed for what has happened to you, and for my ignorance of the truth, and my unjust behavior for doing nothing.

My father had a dream to one day own a cattle ranch; so in 1953, we moved from the city to a farm in Southwest Louisiana. However, he continued to work in the city, driving sixty miles to and from work each day. I attended a very small, rural school. I never saw you or anyone like you at my school, or at the Methodist church we went to in town, or at the grocery store where my mother shopped.

I was an only child and spent a lot of time with my mother. She was a lifetime learner. She read the local newspapers and subscribed to a variety of magazines that she said gave a broader perspective on state, national, and world events. She could speak easily with almost anyone about a number of subjects. She never missed the evening news. In 1960, we watched the Democratic and Republican Conventions. She said she would be voting for John F. Kennedy. Then in January, we watched as he took the oath of office as President of the United States. I'll always remember his famous speech. I liked it so much that Mom bought me a 45 recording of it. In 1963, Mom and I watched Martin Luther King Jr. deliver his "I Have a Dream" speech in Washington, DC. By now, I had seen you in many faces on television; marching, sitting, and standing up for equal rights. Then I watched with horror on television the video of President Kennedy's assassination. It was after this that Congress passed the Civil Rights Act of 1964. Mom said it was long overdue. But the law was tested and I continued to see you standing up, time and time again, to those that would deny you those rights.

In 1967, I started at Northwestern State University in Natchitoches. More than one hundred Black students had enrolled by this time, but it began with only seven courageous students in the spring of 1965. Although I knew you were on campus and attended classes, our paths never crossed. After graduation, I moved to Baton Rouge to attend graduate school at Louisiana State University. Here I saw you in more faces as I walked across campus, or studied in the library, but I didn't make an effort to introduce myself. I want to believe that it was because I was too busy with school and work. The only women I knew well were those that I worked with on campus.

I didn't meet or get to know you until you were the face of the woman who came to my house to care for my young children while I worked. We shared stories about our families, laughed together, and wished each other well; I thought we were friends. Eventually, I moved to Raleigh and you were one of my colleagues. We worked together in human resources, shared stories about our husbands, children, and parents, and attended the same office parties. I thought your struggles to provide a good home and the best for your children were just the same as mine. I thought this for all the years that I worked with you. It took the Black Lives Matter movement to help me begin to appreciate just how different our struggles were. I began to learn; I read books, watched documentaries, went to Civil Rights museums such as those in Montgomery and Jackson, and to interpretative sites that did not gloss over the horrible truths about how my people had hurt you.

I'm so very sorry for the terrible unjust treatment that you, your mother, and the mothers before her endured; and, I admire you more than I can say for your determination and pursuit of what is morally and rightfully yours. America is a better place because of what you have done, but we are not yet where we should be, or where we can be, or where we will be.

Please forgive me. I want to be part of the solution.

How can I help?

Love,
Margaret

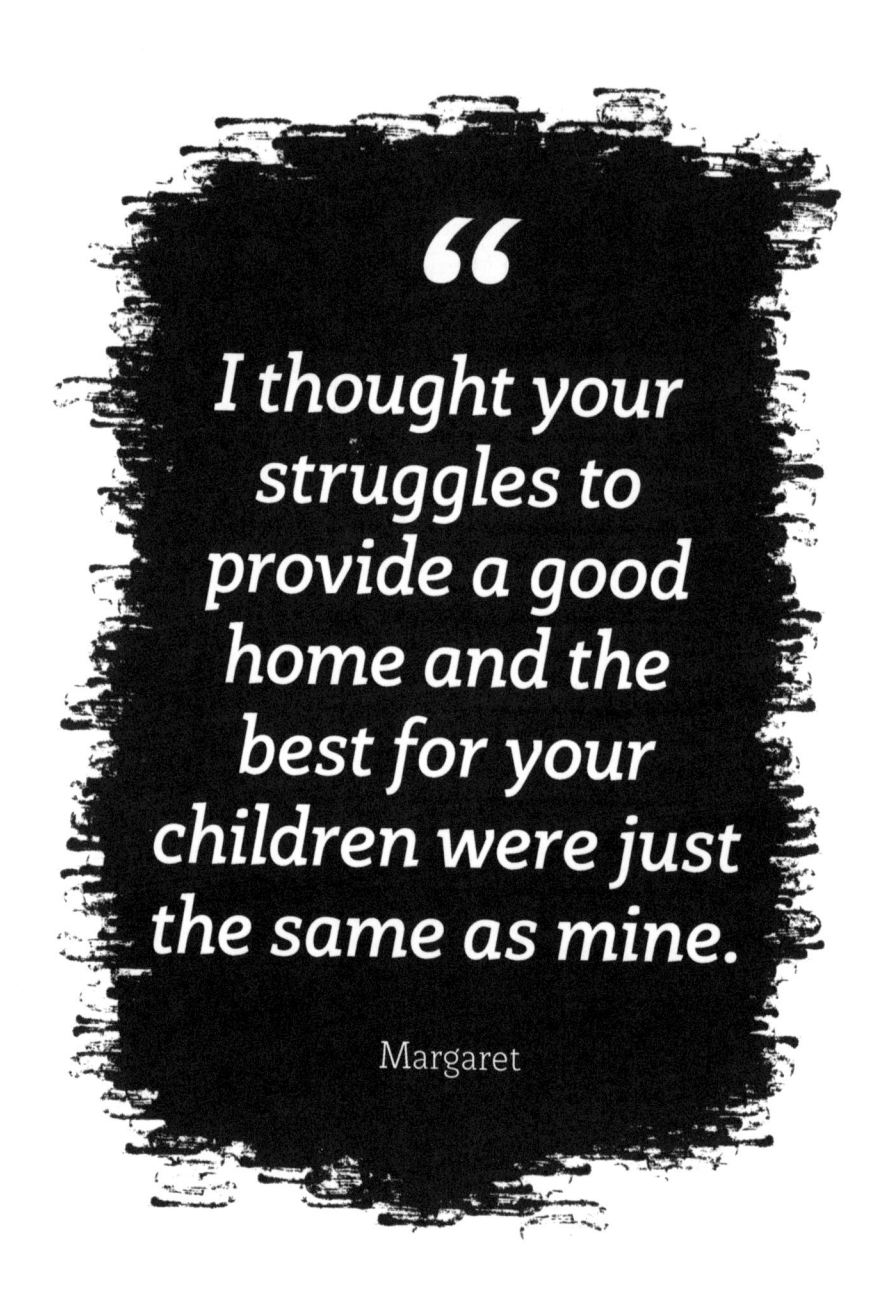

> **I thought your struggles to provide a good home and the best for your children were just the same as mine.**
>
> Margaret

DOING GOOD WITHOUT FEAR

Anonymous

Dear White Woman,

It was a beautiful fall morning, and I was doing my usual walk around the block to get some fresh air and sunlight for the day, especially since the sun was going down earlier. As I was walking, I saw a purse open near a tree, I glanced at it and kept walking deciding to think nothing else of it. As I go into the house, I run upstairs, and my roommate greets me saying "Hey, did you go for a walk?" I told her yes, and that I had just returned. She then inquired, "Did you see the open purse outside?" replied, "Yep, sure did"... She continued, "Yea I looked through it and couldn't find any identification." I paused in awe as I heard her speak so freely without care in such sincerity. I responded "You went through the purse? Just like that without any hesitation?" She said, "Yea, I wanted to see if I could figure out who it belonged to? You wouldn't have done that?"

I looked at my White friend intently, shaking my head in complete candor. No, I wouldn't have. Not only did I not go through the purse, I walked to the other side of the street. It's not because I didn't care about the owner or didn't want it returned. It's because I didn't trust that my good intentions wouldn't be viewed as suspicious. I hesitated because my mind wondered if people would make the wrong presumption or be suspicious of a Black person looking through an empty bag. In that moment I wondered what it was like to not have that hesitation, that fear of people viewing you the wrong way. I wondered what it was like to not have a second thought about a "good act" because you knew you would never be suspected of anything for it. In that moment, as I looked in the eyes of my roommate, even with so many commonalities, she realized that so much of our worldview and even thought processes come from two different worlds. A world where I'm still on the defense, reacting to my environment, shaping and shifting to a framework that wasn't created for me. A world where I still hesitate to do good because of fear.

She looked at me in shock, saddened that this was the lens through which I looked. Sadness is okay, but what I appreciated the most was her openness to understand that my experiences and worldview are different from hers. Her sensitivity and commitment to continually becoming more aware not just of the major ways in which her White privilege exists but the simple day-to-day moments like on that day. That understanding brings a level of sensitivity and awareness to the fact that there are others who have not had that same experience.

So what is my request? I ask that you consider in what ways may your everyday experiences differ from your Black sister. May we all commit to deep, more thought-provoking conversations as we reflect on ways in which the walk in our own shoes differs from one another, so we can walk together more effectively.

– Anonymous
Program Director, Nashville, Tennessee

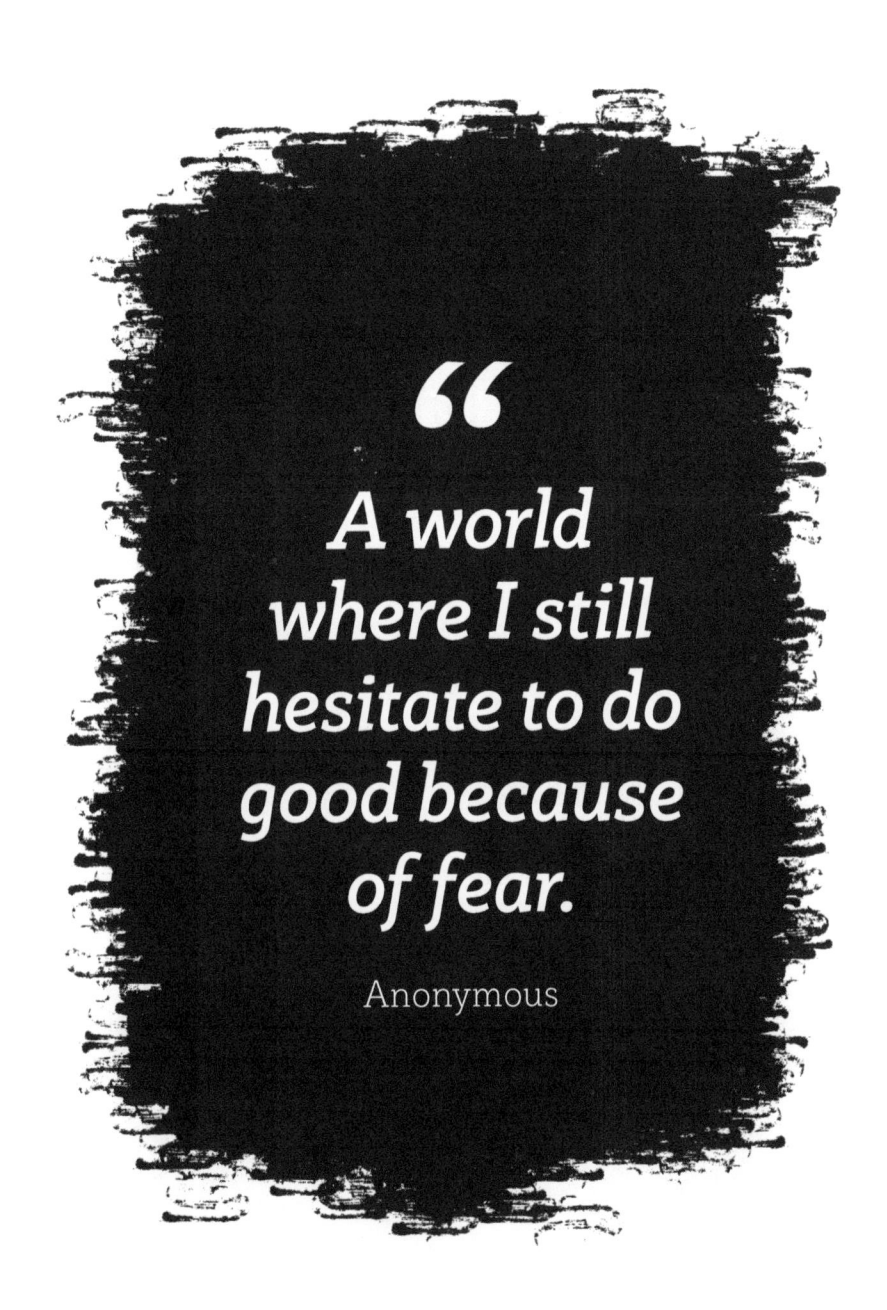

> "A world where I still hesitate to do good because of fear.

Anonymous

BREAKING GENERATIONAL COMPLACENCY

Clare

Dear Black Woman,

This letter is dedicated to Black grandmothers and aunties in my family – through birth and chosen family.

Becoming a mom helped me finally understand why we sing lullabies. I thought they were a bit silly back in my babysitting days. But I know their purpose now. During the late night feedings and the early morning cries, they help both child and caregiver know they are not alone. They soothe. They tell a story.

There is one lullaby that rang especially true this past year after the difficult journey to bring our second baby home. Overwhelmed with the adjustments that come with a newborn, I heard Beyonce sing in Protector, "There's a long line of hands carryin' your name . . . Liftin' you up so you will be raised." It instantly pulled me out of fear and into a higher purpose as I recognized your story in it.

Through the moments of doubt and chaos, I find myself singing this song to teach our little ones that they are part of a family who has loved them long before they were born. You have been preparing their path before I ever became a part of it. You built a home and wealth when the odds were stacked against you. You built a path for these little ones that is much smoother than the one that you had.

I sing this song to remind myself that I am a caretaker of that heritage. I sing it to share your story with the ones I carry. I sing it to ground myself in the duty of stewarding the legacy of Black women who've endured and persisted more than I can imagine. I sing it to honor your love and traditions. I sing it to fortify myself for the responsibility to carry it on.

I'm sure you have had your doubts if I am up to the task, rightfully so. And yet, you have loved me as your own. You have entrusted me with your most precious gift: your legacy.

Ours is an unlikely story. One that my ancestors either thought impossible or reprehensible. Most would have outright forbidden and cursed it. You and I both know that, like most White women in America, I was not raised to honor, understand, or believe your story. Even now, many White women are committed to demeaning or erasing it – from schools and libraries to state legislatures and corner offices. Others condone or perpetuate their peers' actions through apathy or willful ignorance.

So I know that I carry not only our family's legacy, but our country's legacy as well. Our nation's story needs to be rewritten. We need a new legacy to carry on, and we need more caretakers committed to the task. My role in rewriting this story has been to break generational complacency. I'm still rising to meet the level of commitment you have lived. I am still learning the extent to which you have tended to and fought for an abundant vision for your family and nation.

I once heard that a powerful, yet simple prayer is saying, "Thank you." So I offer up this prayer to you. Your friendship, your wisdom, your support – it all has been a gift beyond measure. While I stumble and fail, I am committed to carrying your tradition of raising a legacy. My journey would not have been possible without you – nor would our country.

With Gratitude,
Clare

> *My role in rewriting this story has been to break generational complacency.*
>
> Clare

CLAIMING OUR SPACE AS WOMEN

Koddi

Dear White Woman,

I see you, my white sister.

I see you out here trying to make your way in a world that doesn't always make space for you, doesn't always acknowledge you for who you are, and often doesn't care for you. And I feel that, because I'm right here, walking beside you, down in the trenches, trying to make my way—with steel-toed stiletto boots on, too.
I see you, my sister.

I see you pushing through these new norms, shifting expectations, and breaking barriers in ways that sometimes shock us both as we shock the world. We come across each other often, maybe with hesitation at first, but eventually, we find our way to friendship. And sister, I've learned a lot from you. I've watched how you navigate this space, how you handle yourself when you're up against challenges that just aren't fair.
I appreciate you, my sis.

I appreciate how, time after time, you've lifted me up, been in my corner, rooting for me as I've stepped out to claim my own space. You've been vocal with your support—saying my name in rooms where I wasn't invited but deserved to be. You've used your influence to vouch for my mind. When others shouted me down, through your own tears, you apologized for what they did to us both, all the while pushing me forward. Onward. Up.

We've been through so much together—raising our kids, carrying the scars of life's ups and downs, and doing it all with a kind of grace that doesn't always get celebrated, but is always there.

But I've noticed something else too.

I've watched how you move, how you learn and unlearn, how you grow into different versions of yourself when the world tries to box you in. You're reinventing yourself, refusing to be defined by whatever standard they've declared. And although at times our bonds are strained—worn, torn—I won't focus on that. There are struggles that come with human nature, but we all deserve to survive and thrive. I've seen you act better, so in the low moments, when they seek to divide us, I save space for mutual grace.

Because I've come to realize that there's room for both of us. We don't have to compete or step over one another to get to where we're going. We'll all get there eventually, as long as we work together. Seeing each other. Believing that what's to come is better—deeper, richer.

And so, my friend, I remain hopeful.

I'm in sync with optimism because my 3rd-grade genius daughter has friends of all hues and isn't stopped or swayed by color. I'm hopeful because her best friends come in tones of white, black, brown, and red. I'm hopeful because my daughter and your daughter are living proof that we haven't done everything right, but together, we've made a whole lot of humanity better.

So to my white sister...

My sister...

My sis...

My friend, let's keep going.

Koddi

> "We don't have to compete or step over one another to get to where we're going.

— Koddi

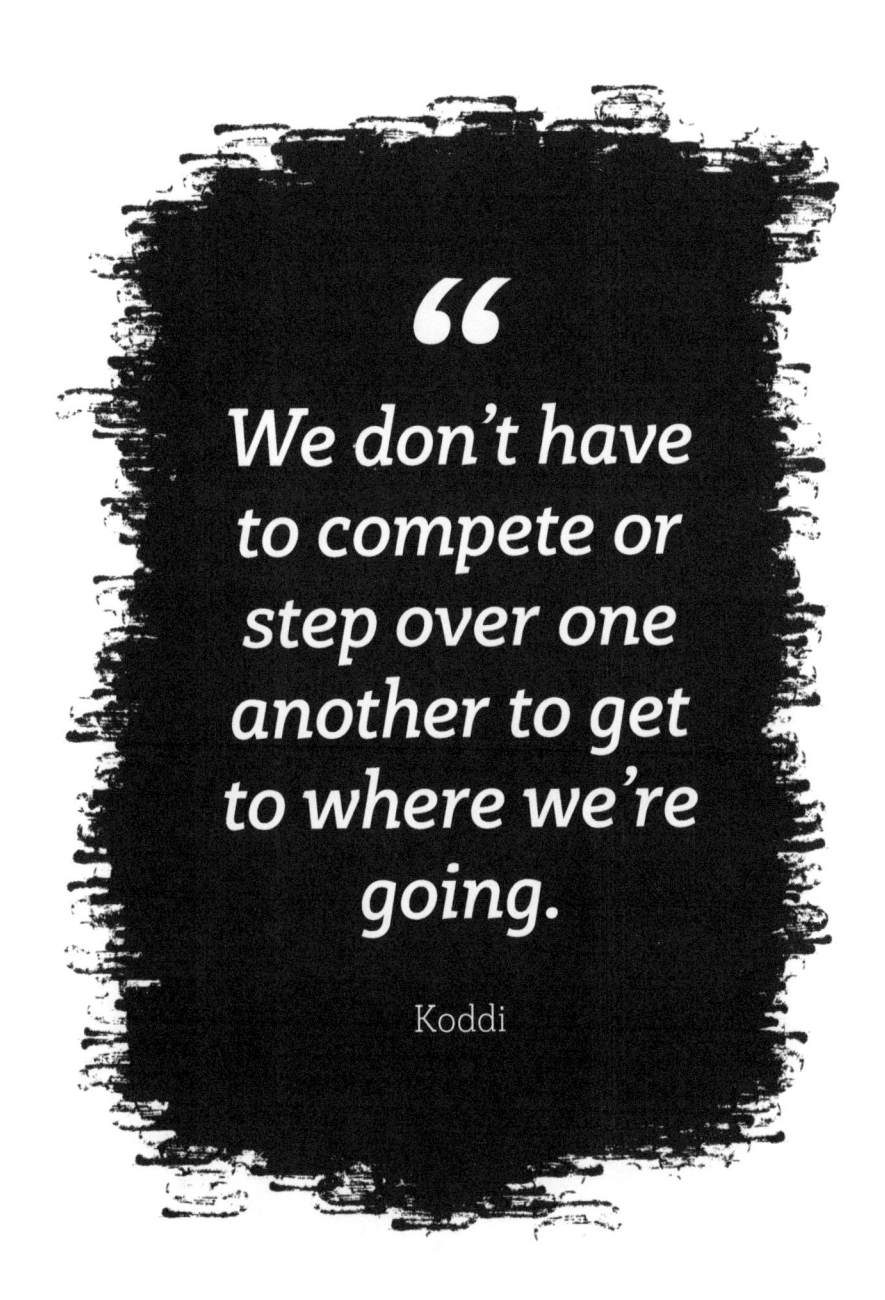

SEEING & CELEBRATING OUR DIFFERENCES

Kristin

Dear Black Woman,

I didn't always recognize my privilege. It wasn't until the murder of Breonna Taylor, and then just a few months later, the murder of George Floyd, that I truly began to focus on my role in racism as a White woman. Their deaths were the last straw – they shattered any illusions I had about the world I lived in. I realized that I could no longer be someone who avoids looking at the harsh realities of racial injustice. Instead, I wanted to be someone who looks, learns, and takes action. This was a turning point for me, igniting a deep desire to educate myself and understand the experiences of Black women so that I could show up differently, not just in words but in actions that catalyze real change.

My initial views of White privilege were naïve, to say the least. I never saw myself as someone with privilege because I didn't grow up "rich." Without the nice cars, big houses, or designer clothes, I believed I wasn't part of the problem. But as I started to dig deeper, I realized how much more complex privilege is. As I learned more about systemic issues like redlining, I began to understand that even something as basic as attending adequately funded schools was a form of White privilege – an advantage I had taken for granted. I had always believed I worked hard for what I have, and I did – but I did it while being White, and that made my path easier in ways I hadn't considered before.

What I've come to understand is that this awareness isn't just about me. It's about seeing you, hearing you, and recognizing the experiences that have been overlooked for too long. It's about acknowledging that the same effort might not have led to the same opportunities if I were a Black woman. I want you to know that this realization is part of a broader movement – one where more and more White women are waking up to these truths and committing to real change. My hope is that, through this journey and by sharing it, we can contribute to a world where your experiences are no longer dismissed but are central to the progress we're striving to make together.

As a White woman, I've encountered moments in predominantly Black spaces where my intentions were questioned, and those experiences have made me reflect deeply on the reasons behind this broken trust. I've seen firsthand how some White women can undermine Black women – whether it's by taking opportunities, advocating for themselves over a Black colleague, or aligning with White men instead of standing in solidarity with Black women. I understand how these actions contribute to a lack of trust. In those moments, I've felt the weight of being judged for what I represent rather than who I am.

This awareness has deepened my understanding of what it truly means to be an ally. It's not about proving myself or trying to fix things; it's about consistently showing up, supporting, and advocating for Black women because I've seen the damage that's been done. My commitment is to rebuild trust and foster a more genuine connection between us through my actions, not just my words.

We are not all the same, and that's the true beauty of the world. To see and celebrate our differences is to embrace what makes life vibrant and meaningful. It's about learning from one another, not swaying one way or the other, but enjoying the richness that comes from diversity. I believe we all benefit when we take ourselves out of the equation and simply appreciate that not everyone is the same.

I envision a world where differences are celebrated and sameness is seen as boring – a world where we are free to make our own choices and live in harmony, respecting and valuing each other. I want you to know that even though change may feel small, it is always positive. You have advocates and allies who stand with you, who are committed to creating a new day. You are not alone in this fight for well-being. I know you're tired, but we're here, ready to work alongside you to bring about the change that's long overdue.

With deep respect and solidarity,
Kristin

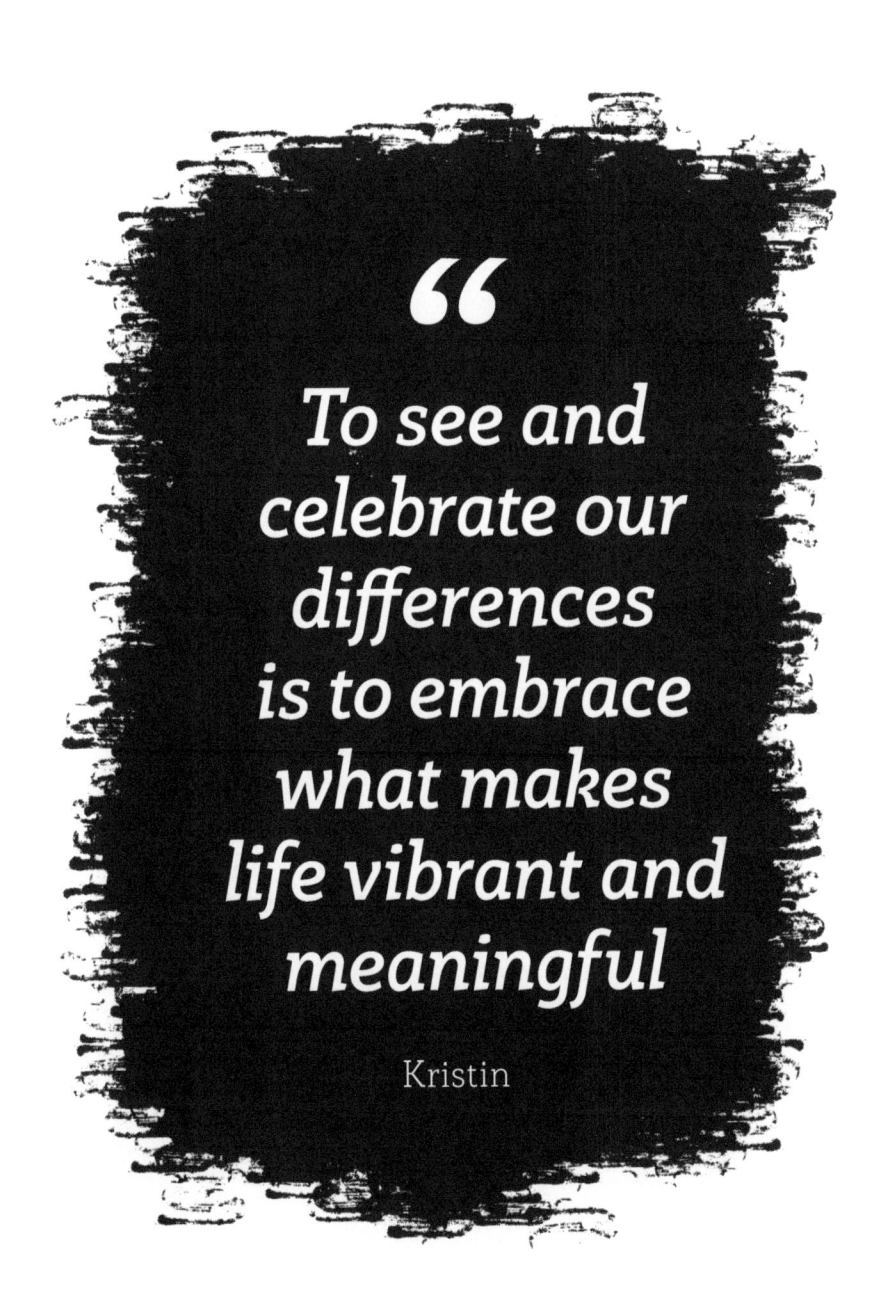

> *To see and celebrate our differences is to embrace what makes life vibrant and meaningful*
>
> Kristin

FINALLY EXHALING

Chantelle

Dear White Woman,

I am a middle-aged, bi-racial, woman with Brown skin inherited from my Jamaican father. I write this letter to you in the spirit of a sisterhood that is beyond space and time, blood and class lines, colour of skin, and even borders created by men. Despite physically being in separate bodies and locations, we must operate from this universal perspective if we are to create a compassionate, just, and inclusive world for all. If we operate from this universal perspective, we will become the authors, rather than mere characters of the collective narrative.

At the same time, we must use our individual bodies, hearts, and minds as agents of change. You, my sisters who embody Whiteness, must not just be allies, but accomplices in rewriting our collective narrative. Let us, your sisters who embody Blackness, feel your loyalty in our bones, so that we know even when we are not with you, you will defend our humanity as though we are standing right next to you.

I met a White-skinned sister, less than a year ago who was younger than me and deeply engaged in the work of correcting the racial prejudice and bias within her, as well as understanding her White privilege. To be honest, I didn't even know this was a thing! I met with her to discuss renting space from her to run some workshops, however our business meeting turned into a life-changing, two-hour conversation. Her fierceness, compassionate heart, and authentic cultural humility caught me off guard. Our interaction evoked a witnessing-healing that caused both of us to cry. She made me feel safe, seen, and understood, like my whole being could finally exhale. This conversation also highlighted all of the times the opposite was true and began to reveal things I had brushed aside in order to not wake up angry every single day; things I needed to heal.

My sisters-in-White-bodies, I ask that you assess the spaces you are in and the company you keep and ask yourself, would my Black- and Brown-skinned sisters feel safe, valued, and respected here? If the answer is no, use your creativity, intelligence, power, and privilege to make it so. Ask your White-skinned friends, "If you knew what you said and did hurt someone, would you want to know and would you stop?" If they answer yes, bring to light their harmful ways. If the answer is no, please guard your heart. No matter how angry or verklempt you may be, keep your heart open and refuse all bitterness that attempts to enter. Resist the urge to make it about 'us' and 'them'. Meet your adversaries exactly where they are, with love, patience, and knowledge. It's better to have a hundred conversations that lead to their epiphany than it is to have one damaging conversation that alienates them from wanting to learn more or do better – although some people do only respond to the latter.

Lastly, please welcome your Black- and Brown-skinned sisters into your homes, into your lives and not just to your causes. I have lost track of how many times I've been invited, from the same women, to speak or participate in events or with organizations to "represent" diversity or a Black perspective – which I'm happy to offer – however, it is starting to grow old. In some cases, I thought a friendship was developing, but I was sadly mistaken. My interaction in these instances never went beyond community-based purposes. I'm beginning to feel like my skin colour combined with my expressiveness is a commodity in the non-profit, liberal world, but who I am as a person and the gifts I have to offer are not as valuable. Tokenism hurts.

I close this letter with a request that you do not be upset at a Black- or Brown-skinned sister if she does not offer acknowledgment of a job well done when you succeed as an accomplice. You are not doing anyone a favour, you are doing what is right. Embodying Blackness on this earthly plane has left your sisters deeply wounded and raw from trauma, as well as extremely tired from fighting for things we shouldn't be fighting for.

Sincerely,
Chantelle

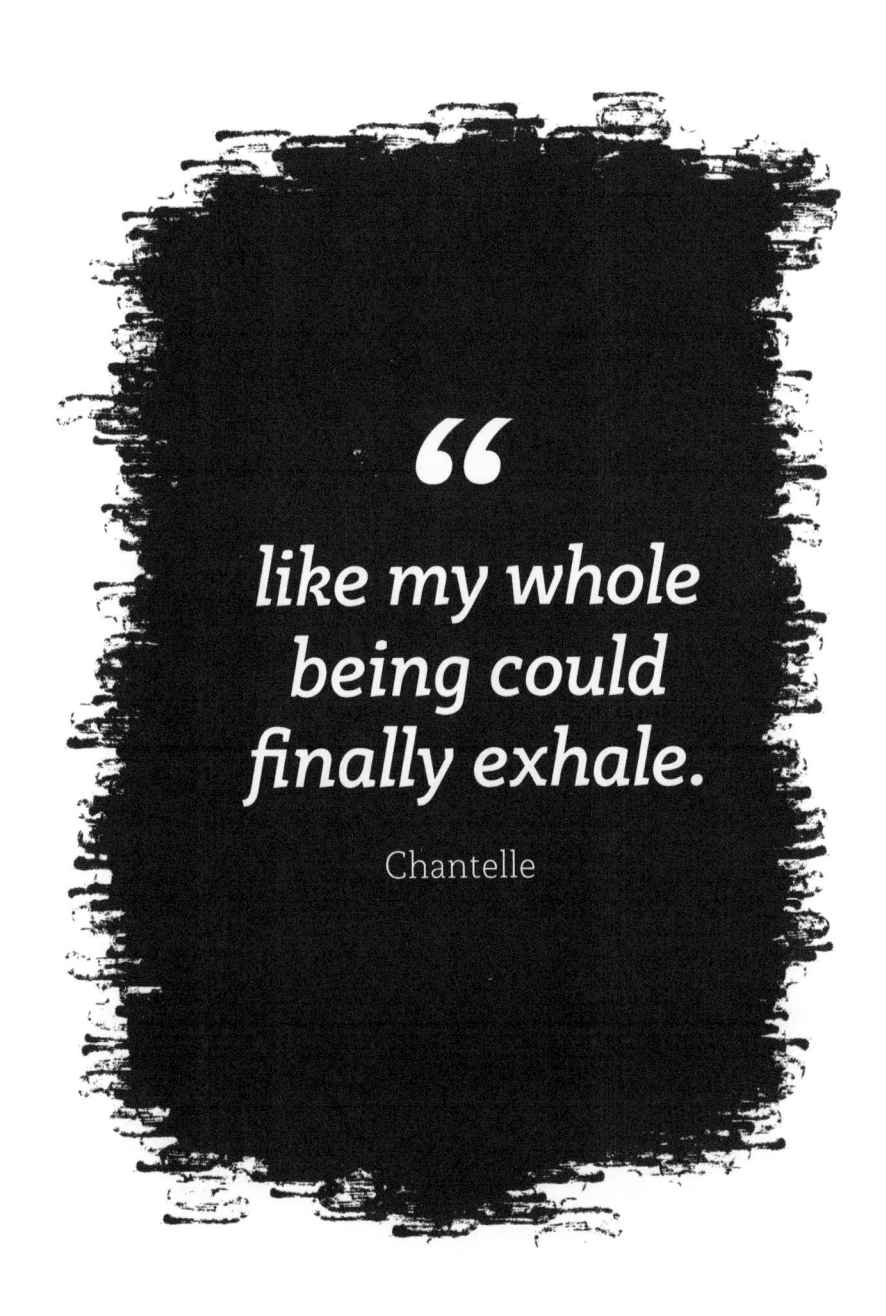

> *like my whole being could finally exhale.*
>
> Chantelle

GETTING UNDER OUR SKIN
―
Dorri

Dear Black Woman,

When we hung out that first time, you said, "All whites are racists." I got so mad my neck burned.

"You don't even know me!" I yelled. "If you did, you'd know I was raised colorblind."

It was your turn to rage: "Don't you know what a cliché that is?"

I didn't.

"Look," I said. "You know nothing about me." On that first outing, we wandered into a Chelsea café. Defensive, I told you I was raised by far-left liberal New Yorkers. It was a home full of music, literature, art. I told you that my parents said, *Don't ever judge anyone by the color of their skin.* All that matters is character. I grew up with dolls from all cultures – Black, Mexican, American-Indian, Asian.

But you weren't having it.

"Listen to yourself!" You railed at me. "Knowing a Black person versus being one is completely different." You ranted about self-loathing. "I hated my dark, Black skin." With eyes blazing, you fired zingers at me. "You're a typical New York Jew," you said, "clueless."

Using every inch of my paltry self-control, I said nothing while sitting there stewing. Suddenly, you saw my upset and softened your tone. Your eyes were watery. "You have no idea what it's like growing up on the south side of Chicago," you told me. "You never ran home as stray bullets whizzed by your head."

That was correct. So, I listened to your story. You were so surprised to find yourself casually chatting with a White couple on a New York subway platform. "I couldn't believe how cool it was," you said. "Just three strangers shooting the breeze."

That is, until the White guy dropped his credit card. You told me you'd been raised with good manners and automatically bent down to retrieve it.

"The White dude's body stiffened with fear," you said. "When I handed it to him, he and his wife looked relieved. They said *thank you*, but their suspicion was typical. My heart fell lower than the subway tracks."

My turn to tear up. Every pain in my life welled up with empathy. Then you said, "All Whites look at us that way."

Seething, I kept my voice low. I hissed, "There's no such thing as all Whites and all Blacks. No Muslims-this and Asians-that." I'd had it. I grabbed my phone off the table, and stomped out.

Had you not called the next day, I would've written you off as an idiot. Instead, we both knew our conversation was unfinished. Thank goodness our desire to understand outweighed our need to be right.

On our second get-together, I felt defensive about my White privilege.

I told you about strangers asking, "What are you?" I say, "A native New Yorker."

"What about your parents?" they ask.

"Philadelphia and New York," I reply.

"But what are you?" they say. "Italian? Spanish?"

"Jewish," I say, "from Russian and Polish Jews who were killed in concentration camps."

Their eyes widen with shock. "What? But you don't look Jewish."
"What do you mean?" I say feigning ignorance.

"Your hair isn't a Jewfro. Your nose is so cute. You seem so. . . normal."

My family has olive skin, dark hair, and dark eyes. I look ethnic. My dad was an Army Captain in World War II. Then and now, I am not from the Aryan race. On forms I choose "other."

Thanks to my parents I learned about using White privilege for activism. Mom has a proudly-framed "thank you" letter from Coretta Scott King. Dad worked in radio – a soul station on AM and pure jazz on FM. Our house was filled with music and visitors of all colors.

Imagine my identity crisis in junior high when I didn't fit in anywhere. Many of my friends were Black, and I found out then about how many people see color. I pretended I didn't hear whispered slurs behind my back.

In 2015, those damn red hats. "Make Germany... er... America Great Again." Friends told me I was overreacting, but I spotted this ghastly rise in White supremacy. Propaganda and pandemic loneliness, but we keep fighting. You and I, and so many others, are on the same page.

We have far more in common than the sum of our differences. I love you.

Your dear friend,
Dorri

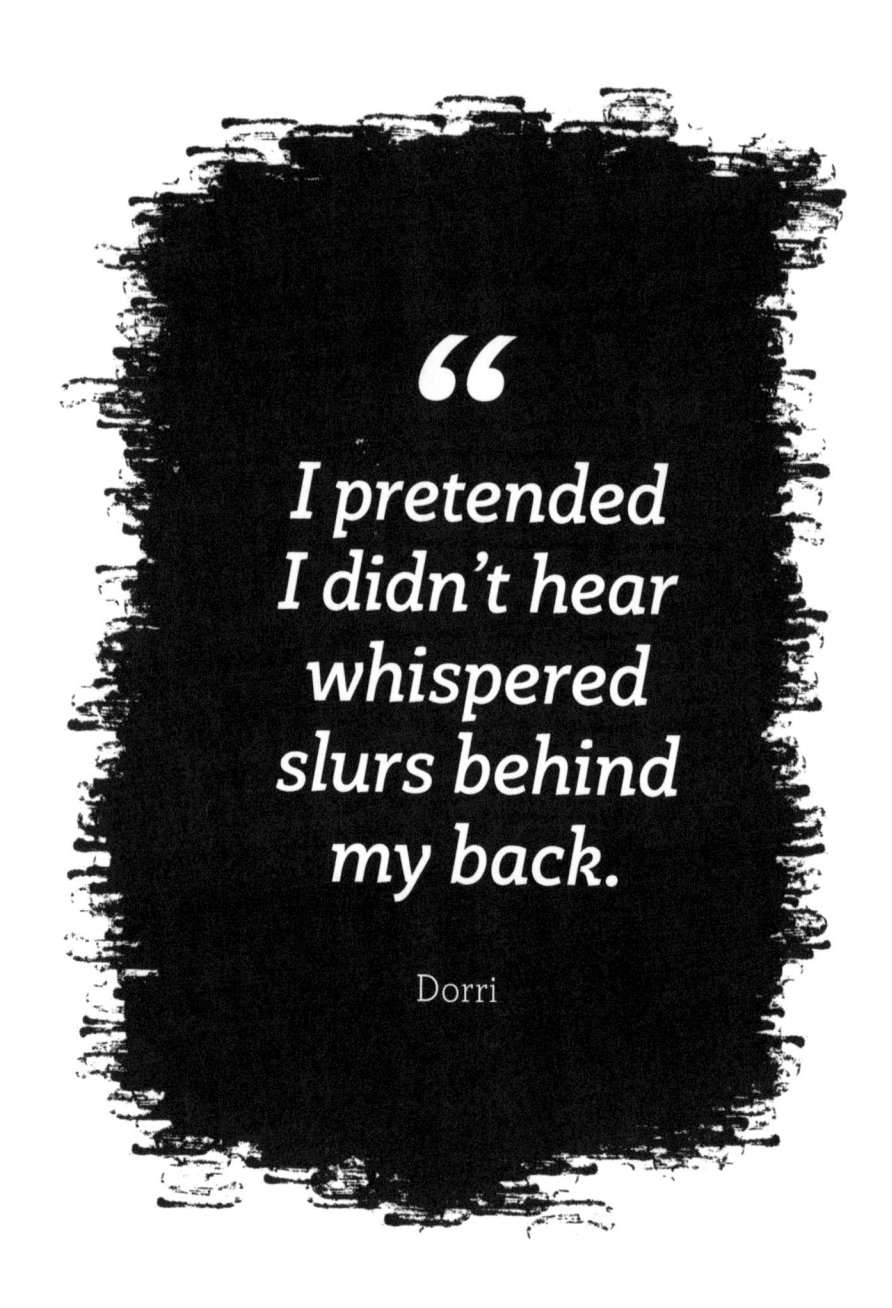

> "I pretended I didn't hear whispered slurs behind my back.

Dorri

A CONCERNED BLACK MOTHER
Aimedra

Dear White Woman,

Like many of you, I am a proud dog mom. Ali has brought immense joy and companionship to our family over the past eight years. He has been a constant presence, joining us for daily walks on the Atlanta Beltline and loyally staying up with my husband during late-night work sessions. Ali doesn't enjoy the dog park though – because he's fiercely protective of me and can't let go of his guard dog responsibilities long enough to have a little fun. It's been wonderful watching him grow alongside my children, and his bond with them is something truly special. Even now, as both of my kids are away at college, their first question during every call is always, "How's Ali?"

Yet, despite all this joy, there's a stark contrast in our experiences. Unlike many of you, I didn't initially want a dog. My career, my marriage, raising two children, and settling into our new home had already filled my plate to the brim. I was spread thin, barely able to carve out any time for myself. But life, as it often does, had other plans. My son was approaching his thirteenth birthday, a milestone that should have been filled with excitement and hope for the future. Yet I found myself overwhelmed with a sense of dread. In this country, I knew that the world was about to shift for him in ways it wouldn't for other boys his age. I didn't know exactly when it would happen, but I knew the time was approaching when society would stop seeing my son as the joyful, kind child he is and start viewing him as a threat.

I saw the shift happen too often, and I feared for the day it would come for him. It wasn't just an abstract fear. It was rooted in the daily realities of being a Black mother in America. I knew the simple act of walking through our own neighborhood might one day become dangerous for him – not because of anything he did, but because of the way he would be perceived. So, in a desperate bid to protect him, I decided to get a dog. You might be wondering how the two things are connected. For me, it was an act of strategy – an attempt to create a buffer. Since my White neighbors appeared to care more about dogs than young Black men, I thought if I armed my son with a golden doodle, he would be safe as he roamed the streets of his neighborhood. Maybe then, he wouldn't be seen as a threat. Maybe then, people would see him as the boy he was rather than the shadow of danger they imagined him to be.

There is something profoundly terrifying about being the mother of a Black son in this country. It is a fear that stays with me, lingering at the back of my mind whenever he leaves the house. This is not a fear I wish upon anyone, and I don't want you to have to carry it. But I do want you to understand it. I want you to see what it means to love someone so deeply and yet to live with the constant anxiety that the world might not love them back. When you see a Black man, I want you to see more than just a suspect. I want you to think of him as you would your own son, your nephew, your grandson. Imagine the weight of that love and the fear of losing it in an instant.

Sincerely,
Aimedra, a Concerned Black Mother

> "There is something profoundly terrifying about being the mother of a Black son in this country."
>
> — Aimedra

TURNING THE PAGE
Kacie

Dear Black Woman,

Is it more important to be prolific or honest?

Today, I argue the latter.

I have started this letter no less than eight, now nine, times. Instead of worrying that I get it right, I'm going to just get it started; and, I hope that more White women take that same cue.

The first iteration of this letter was a jotted-down thought in my journal from years ago. It starts:

Dear Black Woman - I love watching you thrive. Your Black girl magic is meant to be in the spotlight. And this is your moment.

Admittedly, I did not see the depths of your contributions before the 2016 election. Unlike you, it was then that I first felt the threat of what it means to have your rights questioned; and so, it was also the first time I cared. And for that, I'm sorry.

It's no secret that I love women. But, over the past few years as I've gone on my own inward journey, and also watched as our country has faced both racial and political reckonings I came to completely revere Black women – overrun with admiration, adoration, and awe.

TURNING THE PAGE

Stacey said, "Like most who are underestimated, I have learned to over-perform." Yep, I feel that. I am not you, but I am in awe of you. I want to learn and work alongside you so that it's not just a world better for women, but it's a world better for Black women. It's my responsibility to know that difference, and I do.

Black Lives Matter. Black is beautiful. Shop black, buy Black. F*ck, yes. I see you, beautiful women. I am here to listen and amplify your voices. 'Cause you've been saying and doing a lot without an audience.

Well, now you have an audience, and we're here to follow your lead.

I read it back and feel all the same overwhelm of admiration and hope; a sense that we were turning a page. I, too, feel overwhelmed with how naive I was to think it'd be so easy. I now know more intimately than ever before, change takes time, and progress isn't linear.

I say that to you here, and you probably say, *"Right."*

As a White woman, I think that's the thing I'm learning. It's not that our lot in life isn't without struggle, but that our struggle has a lot more autonomy and alternative paths to get out of them, simply by inhabiting our White bodies. It wasn't until the 2016 election that I fully realized the depths of what it means to be dismissed by society, by our government, by people I loved and thought would protect me. I won't speak for you, but I imagine that those are feelings you know well. And the sheer energy required to keep showing up when so many just want you to go away is exhausting.

I often wonder what kind of utopia we'd be living in if we collectively didn't have to spend so much time, energy, and capacity fixing what someone else broke.

I don't want to be patronizing; saying what I think I should say because a Black woman will read my White words, and I want to be seen as 'one of the good ones.' I can't say if I'm a 'good one.' What I can say though, is that I have deep respect and admiration for your experience, perspective, and expertise.

Simply by the body you occupy and the way you've moved through this world of ours, you know more than I do. I don't pretend to want to have to embody the strength or experiences you have. Instead, the best way I know to pay it forward for your far-reaching contributions is to listen when you talk, follow when you lead, and offer coverage when you rest.

Let me sign off by saying, I'm standing beside you, shoulder to shoulder, ready to take your lead. You know, as you always have, what to do next. Not because of some position of privilege you were born into, but because of all the privileges you weren't.

Here's to you, Black Woman.

Your White Sister,
Kacie

> " *a sense that we were turning a page.*
>
> Kacie

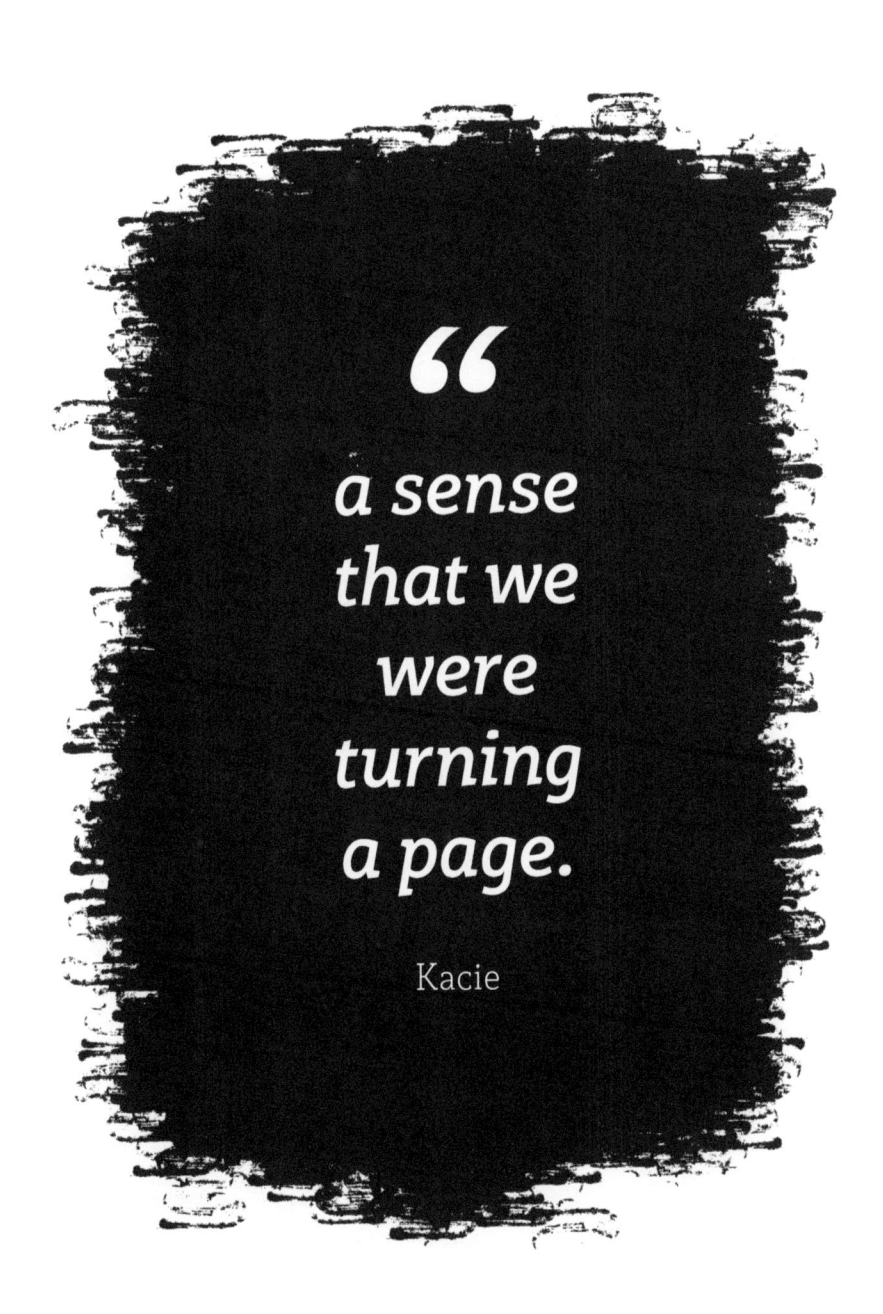

PULLING SCALES OFF YOUR EYES
—
Antoinette

Dear White Woman,

I recall sitting in a Social and Cultural Diversity class at the former Argosy University almost a decade or so ago. The class was a mix of about half and half – half White and half Black that is. We were discussing "White privilege." As you can see these discussions were being had long before the Breonna Taylor's, Sandra Bland's, and countless others. I remember us talking specifically about how historically, Whites hindered the purchase of land by Blacks. Yes! There was a time in recent history where Blacks could not own land, at least not of significant value. I recall one of my classmates, who was a White female, bursting into tears during the discussion. Our professor paused for a moment to allow us all to process. What happened in that moment was an awakening. My classmate attempted to share through the tears, that she had never been exposed to such truth and felt horrible that she had been so naïve.

While several years have now passed, that moment still resonates with me. I have often heard it said, and I find myself saying it often, "Knowledge is power, while ignorance remains a very blissful place." This still rings true years later, especially as it relates to White privilege. I have engaged in countless conversations over the past few years with colleagues, family, friends, and the like, around the absence of knowledge in this space. If only others would assume the position of my classmate on that night in class, opening and allowing herself to be vulnerable, would we see impactful change.

I assume you are a White woman reading this message, and it is my sincerest hope and prayer that you will not wait until someone comes along to pull the scales off of your eyes, but that you snatch them off yourself – even if it hurts – to allow you to see the hurt that we as Black women live daily. If each one of us will reach one, accept what reality is, and do our part to influence others, then we can see real change. I have been telling those that I have been engaging that this is a matter of the heart. Jeremiah 17:9 says, "The heart is deceitful above ALL things and beyond cure. Who can understand it?" This scripture speaks volumes regarding the issues we deal with.

Let's not let the life of Justice Ruth Bader Ginsburg be in vain. She fought until the bitter end for not just the liberation of women, but ultimately all. Women are the givers of life and are the conduit God uses to bring creation to earth. That alone shows the power we possess. Let's use it for good! God loves you and so do I!

In His Love,
Antoinette
Atlanta, Georgia

> *pull the scales off of your eyes*

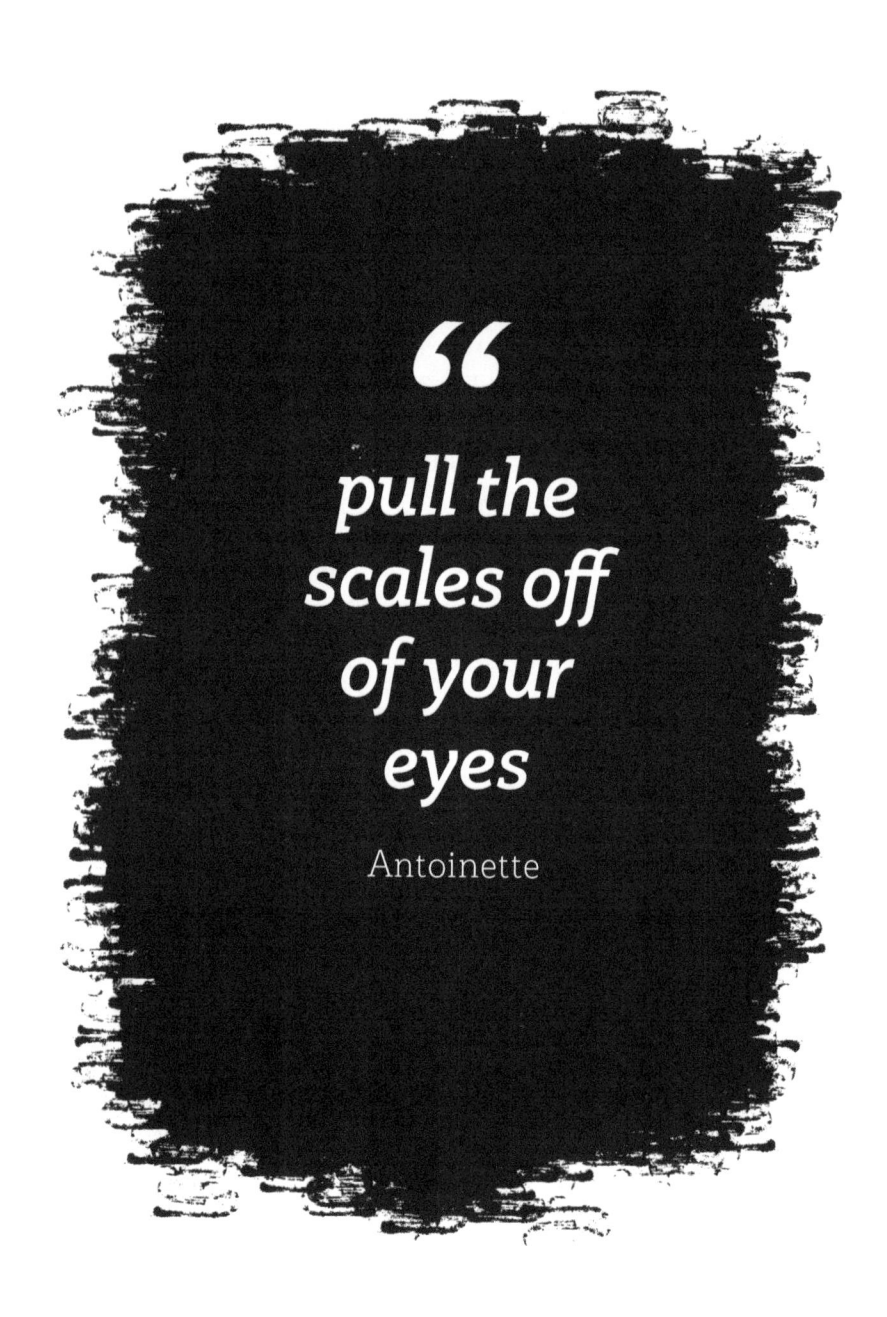

— Antoinette

LINKING ARMS AS YOUR SISTER

Kathy

Dear Black Woman,

It's taken me almost fifty years to write this letter. More than fifty years ago, I was a student at a religiously affiliated university in the South. I came to school in 1967, the same year a young Black student was graduating from the university. The student was famous, not for his grades or accomplishments, which were many, but because he had been refused entry into the church that sat at the corner of the university campus. A year later, I sat in a pew in a small clapboard church in the middle of nowhere, listening to the words of a young Black preacher from Atlanta as he talked about racial injustice and his plan to move us all toward Beloved Community.

I failed you and I failed myself, and I am here to say *I'm sorry*. For fifty years, I have done nothing to move us – you and I – to the place where I can look at you across a table and know that I have done my best to heal the wounds, to make amends, to link my arm through yours as your sister, your ally, and your friend.

For years, I have watched the back and forth between White

supremacy and social injustice and shoved it all aside as work for someone else to tackle. Many times, I would think to myself, *When are THEY going to do something to turn gerrymandering or redlining around? When are African Americans, Latinos, and Asians going to get with the program and work to be more like me?*

Ahmaud Arbery changed all that for me.

I watched in rapid succession as Brianna Taylor and George Floyd joined Ahmaud and paid the price of racial hatred and bigotry. I watched young people fill the streets. I watched signs telling me that Black Lives Mattered and reminding me what it might be like not to be able to breathe. And I got sick – sick to my stomach, sick in my heart, and sick right down to my soul for all the ways I had failed to speak up, to speak out, to make a difference.

What one thing did I know for sure, as Oprah would ask me. I knew that the only way to make a difference was to open my door, to spread my table, and to have open and honest dialog – about the things I didn't know, about the ways I didn't understand, about laws that held us back and those that moved us forward. I knew that I wanted, no, that I needed to know you, and I needed for you to know me. I knew that I needed to learn to lean in and listen better. And I knew that Maya Angelou might be whispering in my ear, "Kathy, you know better, now it's time to do better."

How am I doing that? I opened a Zoom account and I grabbed the most popular book on racism I could find. I called all of my friends and told them it was time to have a study session. We began later that year, and we're still reading and learning. Our circle has widened and there are now faces of all colors in our book group. I am working with my church and facilitating a wonderful discussion on the history of racism and the Christian's role in helping heal a great divide. I will soon be teaching a course on racism for adult students through the university at which I worked. I'm introducing Civic Dinner conversations into my community. And still it's not enough.

So let me say what I should have said at the beginning:

I am sorry. I'm sorry that it's taken me so long.

I promise. I promise to remember what price you and your ancestors have paid to build this country.

I pray. I pray for the day when we may find peace together and see Beloved Community.

And I hope. I hope that you will one day, look across a table at me and we'll both smile, knowing that each in our own way has done what we could to make this country and this world a better place.

Journeying together,
Kathy

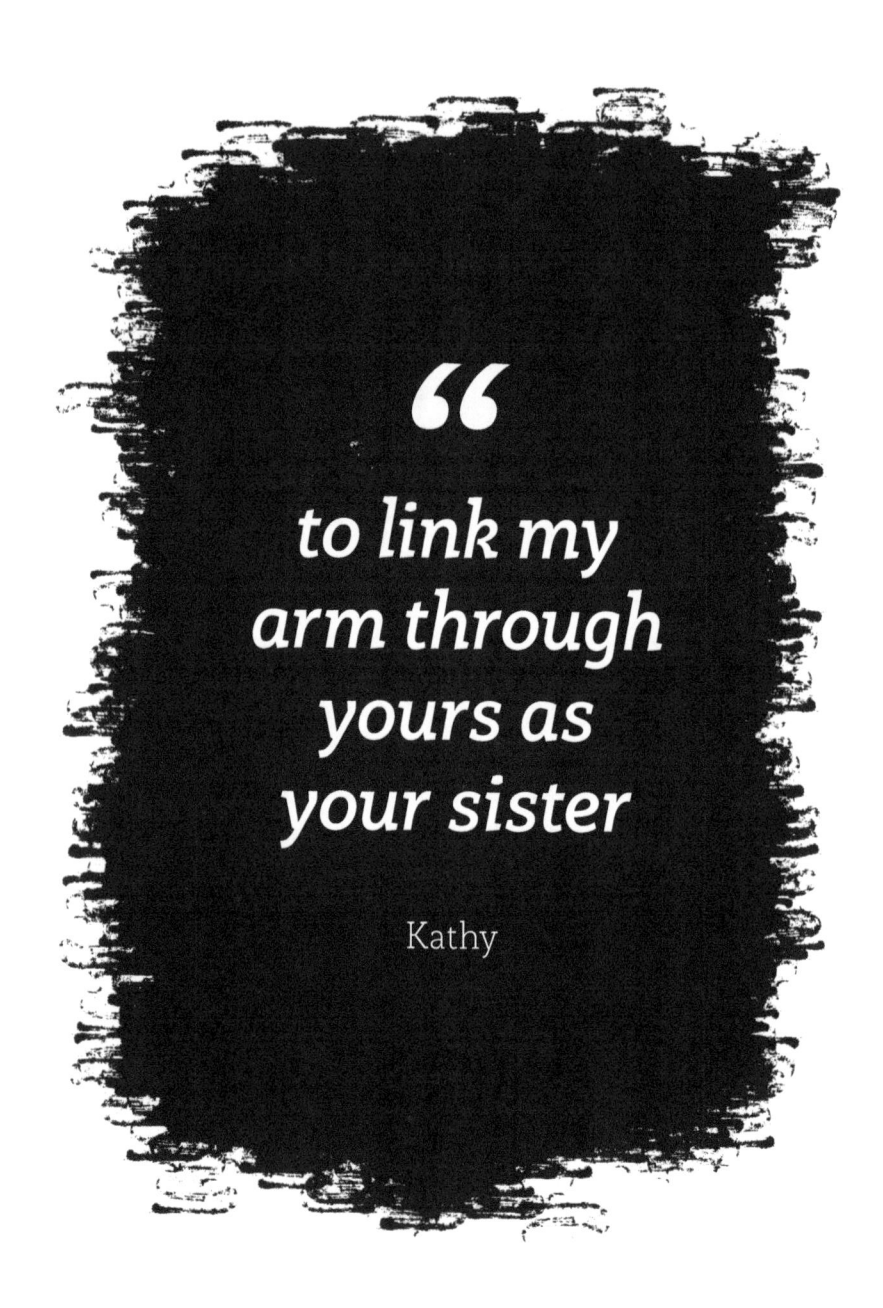

> "to link my arm through yours as your sister
>
> Kathy

BLACK WOMEN DREAM OF BEING MOTHERS TOO

Julianne

Dear White Woman,

More Likely To Die. I admitted the patient on a Thursday. By Friday, she was gone. Sickle cell disease in pregnancy is not a good mix, even in an otherwise healthy, fit, and beautiful Black woman as she was. Health disparities, coupled with inequities of and access to healthcare, have birthed an exhaustingly true reality: Black women in America are *more likely to die.*

As a women's health specialist for the past twenty years, part of my life's work entails keeping my patients from becoming statistics of disparate morbidity and mortality. Promotion of health and wellness should be the foundation of our American healthcare system. Our foundation, however, is compromised and has instead become a machine built to manage disease and to, with all our might, delay premature death. Still, one thing has been clear to me: you and I share common goals no matter our ethnicity, geography, or economy. Women – whether coupled or single, mothers or not – we want to love and be loved as deeply, as fully, and as long as we can. When I attended my patient's funeral at the invitation of her family, I vowed even more so to help the women I care for to attain this one core goal and human right.

According to the U.S. Centers for Disease Control and Prevention (CDC), Black women are three times *more likely to die* during pregnancy, childbirth or up to a year after. Kira Johnson, Torie Bowie, Dr. Chaniece Wallace – these are just a few names once plastered in headlines. They were Black women who died and shouldn't have. The CDC has warned that deaths like these were and are preventable. Consequently, there are young Black women who now think twice about starting or expanding their families.

There are even more alarming rates of near-misses – almost four for every one maternal death. Black women dream of being mothers too. They deserve to be discharged from the hospital swaddling their newborns. Even celebrities such as Beyonce and Serena Williams have shared their own harrowing birthing stories and when they speak, we sit up, and listen. Perhaps it influenced then Senator Kamala Harris to champion a landmark legislative package known as the Black Maternal Health Momnibus Act along with Representatives Lauren Underwood (D-OH) and Alma Adams (D-NC) in 2020. A growing list of leaders in Washington, D.C., have lent their support to address this plight from every angle possible. A few of these include confronting structural racism in healthcare, expanding Medicaid up to one year postpartum in all states, and growing a diverse perinatal workforce for women living in maternity care deserts (https://Blackmaternalhealthcaucus-underwood.house.gov/Momnibus).

More likely to die. White women are actually more likely to be diagnosed with breast cancer than Black women. According to Susan G. Komen, studies show that White women are more likely than women of some other ethnicities (including Black and Hispanic women) to have children at a later age, to have fewer children, and to use menopausal hormone therapy. These factors are linked to an increased risk of breast cancer. So why are Black women *more likely to die?* Studies are underway, but it appears that some risks lie in the fact that Black women overall are diagnosed at a younger age and have more aggressive diseases than our counterparts. In fact, Inflammatory Breast Cancer and Triple Negative Breast Cancer (TNBC) are found more often in Black women and are more lethal. TNBC carries a small increased risk in this population who also tends not to breastfeed and may carry excessive weight in their abdomens. It is disheartening that we are leaders in ways we wish not to be.

Speaking of leading, Black women have higher rates of just about every chronic health condition there is. Diabetes, heart disease, hypertension, anemia, obesity – shall I go on? Basically, a risk factor for disease in America is, well, being Black in America. And when our society plays down the impact of American history – think slavery, the Civil Rights era, the Tuskegee Syphilis Study, Covid-19 – we get more than just insulted. We actually can become ill. So, while governmental and health agencies can spew stats and facts regarding declining numbers of certain conditions like a decrease in cervical cancer, breast cancer, heart disease, etc., we as Black women are *still more likely to die.*

And even more eye-opening is how being a double minority in America affects us. As published in the February 2021 *Journal of Women's Health*, this intersection of race and gender for Black women is more than the sum of being Black or being a woman: it is the synergy of the two. Black women are subjected to high levels of racism, sexism, and discrimination at levels not experienced by Black men or White women. Hmph! So, when we call out Black Girl Magic or speak about your privilege, understand, my White sister, it is for us to feel inclusivity in a system that minimizes our existence.

As a little girl, I sang in the youth choir at my church. "Red and yellow. Black and white. They are precious in His sight," I sang with a feeling of hope. Yet, I understood that America spoke of equality with exceptions. So, if you have a friend, neighbor, co-worker, or fellow PTA mom who is a Black woman, I implore you to see her with a different lens. As she is fighting for her own health and wellness, know it is possible, that she is also shouldering the burden of her partner or spouse, children, aging parents, and oftentimes, more. For certain, we are not a monolith. But social, economic, and educational factors pushed aside, we are still Black with risks we inherently carry that cause us to stay on top of a leaderboard we want no parts of – *More Likely To Die.*

Wishing you well,
Julianne
Board-certified Obstetrician/Gynecologist

> **Black women dream of being mothers too.**
>
> Julianne

FACING THIS WORLD TOGETHER

Tamara

Dear Black Woman,

There is a wave of conflicting emotions running through my head as I open this letter. I want to be honest, share my respect and love, and provide value with my thoughts. Yet, there is an underlying guilt, shame, and anxiety that gives me pause, and sometimes results in silence.

This tends to be the way it goes with my relationships with Black women. I pride myself on being progressive and open-minded, but I also have become painfully aware of my ignorance and baked-in prejudices and biases. These sometimes result in actions and thoughts that are more to protect my fragile sense of self, security, and pride, rather than truly being present and holding space for my Black sisters.

I grew up in an almost exclusively White town in central New York. I didn't know of any blatant racism, but I also was totally oblivious to the systemic and pervasive racism that is steeped in our society. I was privileged and clueless.

In college, I was fortunate enough to have been taught by James Farmer, the famed Civil Rights activist who marched alongside

Martin Luther King Jr. My mind was broken open. Stories and history were presented in a way I had never heard before, for the first time, I honestly was able to look at and understand the struggles and triumphs of Black people. The feeling crept up that I wished I was something else than a middle-class White Anglo Saxon Protestant (WASP). I felt like I was missing out on having a sense of connection and allegiance with others like me, others who face the same battles and sing the same victory songs.

As I have gotten older, I realize that I have an allegiance and connection with all women, despite our different races, backgrounds, and religions. This connection and sisterhood brings me joy and purpose and has helped me to look into my biases and to form authentic bonds with my Black women friends. I hope that you know that I will use my privilege to be your voice if necessary, to risk losing some of my privilege if it means gaining some for you.

Becoming a mother of two boys and having Black mother friends, learning about "the talk" ... this is the point that my heart completely broke open. My sons and your sons live in different worlds.

My responsibility extends beyond our relationship, it now extends to teaching my boys about their privilege, to help them understand how their Black friends have to move differently in this world. We must learn about anti-racism and the importance of being uncomfortable and acknowledging that we all have racist thoughts and beliefs – not to cause us shame, but to fully understand we are steeped in this racist world – it is in the air we breathe and the water we drink. We must learn to have empathy for others and confront our human faults.

And I thank you, my Black woman friend, for being so strong. For being the one who continues to do the *hard damn work* to lead us towards progress. For being the beautiful Queen whom I can look to for inspiration. Thank you, and I hope to do better by you and your children – by teaching my children to use their privilege in a way that betters the world for everyone, not just their White boy selves.

But here I am, realizing that this whole letter has been about me. Soothing my conscience, explaining away my faults, and making sure that you understand that I am doing the best I can. Making myself feel good and secure.

Back to the push-and-pull of this complicated dance. This is not all about me. I want to ask for grace and patience, but at the same time, I realize how f*cked up it is for me to be asking **you** for grace – to hold my fragile little heart carefully so that I feel good about myself.

So, in the end, I don't ask for anything from you except the chance to laugh with you when things are funny, hike with you when the weather is gorgeous, cry with you when things get to be too much, and stand beside you as we face this world together.

Love,
Tamara

> *stand beside you as we face this world together*
>
> Tamara

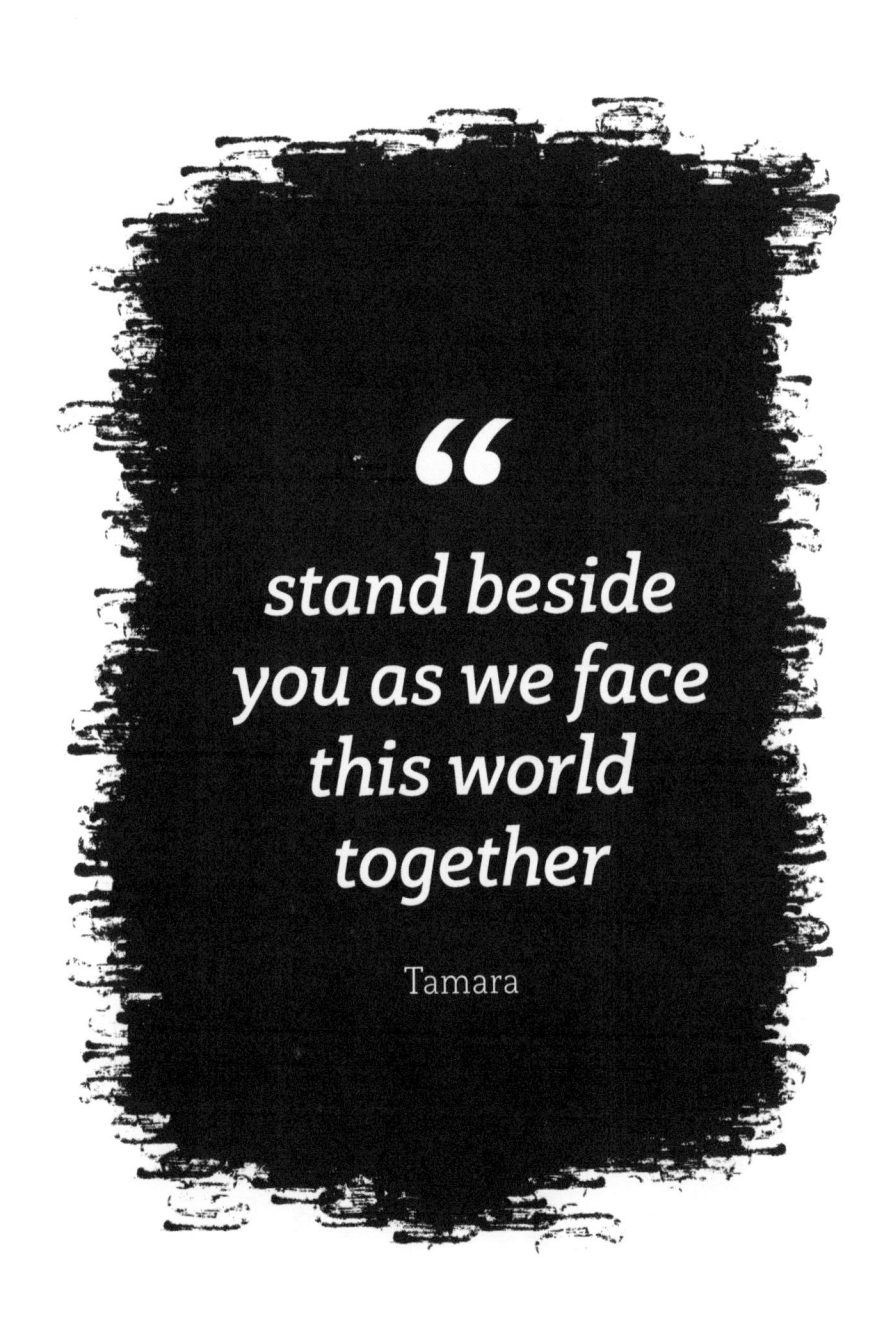

BELIEVE OUR TRUTH

Ekaette

Dear White Woman,

I need you to believe me when I say I have been discriminated against – not question, not doubt, but believe.

As a Black woman, I have often been perceived as less human, as stronger than I should need to be, and somehow more deserving of abuse while better equipped to handle it. It's a dehumanizing cycle I've lived with, and I want to share a story with you that shaped my understanding of this harsh reality.

I was the first Black woman to serve as the society editor for *Charleston Magazine*. If you know Charleston, South Carolina, you know it's a city that still grapples with its history of slavery and racism. As society editor, I attended the city's prestigious galas, philanthropic events, and social gatherings – spaces that historically weren't designed with someone like me in mind. I knew, walking into these rooms, that I would not be greeted with open arms. But I could never have imagined the depths of what I would experience.

At one event during the Spoleto Festival, I was asked to enter through the back entrance. No one gave a reason – it was simply expected that I comply. I've been called out of my name, mistaken for another Black woman editor at the magazine, despite our skin tones, hair, and facial features being nothing alike. Yet, it seemed that to some, we were indistinguishable – just Black women.

I shared these stories with my White friends. And you know what? They didn't believe me. They told me I was overreacting, that I was seeing things that weren't there. The hurt and anger I felt were overwhelming. I felt unheard, unseen.

It wasn't until one day, when a good friend of mine witnessed it firsthand – watching me be repeatedly called the other woman's name at an event – that she finally believed me. She had to see it to believe it.

But here's the thing: I shouldn't need proof for my experience to be valid. Black women shouldn't need to justify our pain for you to understand that it's real.

So, dear White woman, I ask you to trust us when we speak our truth. Know that our experiences are real, even if they are uncomfortable or outside your lived reality. Listen to us, believe us, and stand with us. We are fighting to be seen as fully human, just as you are.

With hope,
Ekaette

> *Black women shouldn't need to justify our pain for you to understand that it's real.*

Ekaette

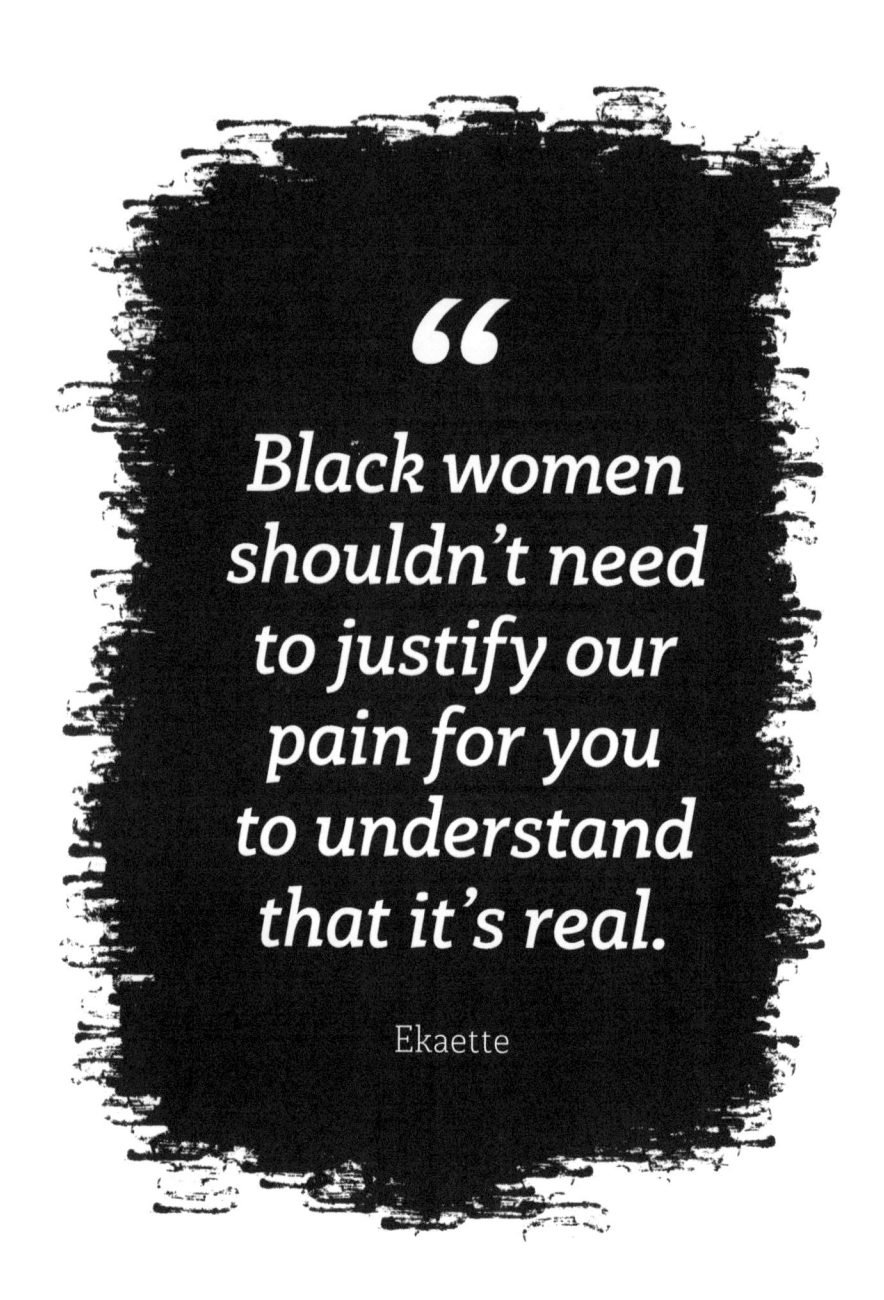

FLY IN THE BUTTERMILK

Betsy

Dear Black Woman (Sister),

I want to tell you about a few moments that have taught me some important life lessons.

My parents moved to Virginia when they were newly married. They had left a White community, being White themselves. There was a gentleman of color who lived upstairs who briskly invited them over for drinks. They declined the drinks, but were happy for the invite and joined him for the evening. As they were visiting, he offered them some tobacco; they also declined smoking due to religious beliefs. He kindly accepted their oddity by saying, "Well, peoples got to be people".

They ended up becoming dear friends. After my parents moved back to Utah they lost contact with him. He is unaware that his words became impactful and often used by my family.

At seven years old, my family traveled east for my father's job. During the seven-day drive, we took many breaks. I spotted a girl about my age in fluffy pigtails at a stop. We had a great time playing together. She was the first Black child I had ever met in person. I remember her laugh sounding like jingle bells on a cold winter day. Her smile was kind and sincere and her eyes twinkled like the stars. As my family started to drive away though, I started to think about some things. Recently I had learned about the history of African American people at school and realized at once that it was people who looked like me that had hurt people who looked like her. The division in my mind was immediate. There was instant shame for what my skin represented. Little did I know that the injustice hadn't ended with my ancestors.

As a young adult, I lived in Kentucky for a short time. At church one Sunday I was sitting by a dear friend. She whispered to me, "It looks like I'm the only fly in the buttermilk." She was making a joke about her dark skin. In a room of about thirty women, she was the only woman of color. I was shocked, I hadn't even noticed! I guess that would be an example of White privilege. Not having to notice the difference. I didn't know what to say. I ended up saying something dumb like; everybody likes chocolate in their milk, if anything you are the chocolate! That day, I became aware of my ignorance in not knowing what to say to make my friend feel the connection of sisterhood.

Years later, living back in Utah I was helping in a P.E. class. There was a student who was acting out badly; it was unlike him to have this kind of behavior. I pulled him aside to find out what was going on. He proceeded to tell me that he and his mother had been watching the news the previous night. The report was about children shopping for dolls. Both Black and White children were only buying dolls with light skin. The report was in an attempt to bring awareness but backfired horribly for this young man. After the report ended, his mother, in trying to prepare her son for the future of being a Black man in America did her best to explain this "awareness" to him. His innocence was crushed and he felt unwanted which resulted in his current aggressive behavior. I tried to comfort him and reassure him that he was adored. I reminded him that he got picked first at school often. And he had many friends who picked him to be their buddy on their own. Unfortunately, the damage was already done. It took one news report! One, to destroy the positive image he had had of himself previously. I often wonder how he is now.

In conclusion, I want my black friends to know:
    1. You are **never** the fly in the buttermilk!
    2. I would pick a Black baby doll every time, hands down!
    3. You are adored and you are respected.

My call of action is for us to work together to bridge
our disconnect.

After all – "Peoples gotta be people" – and I believe we can become dear friends.

Your friend,
Betsy

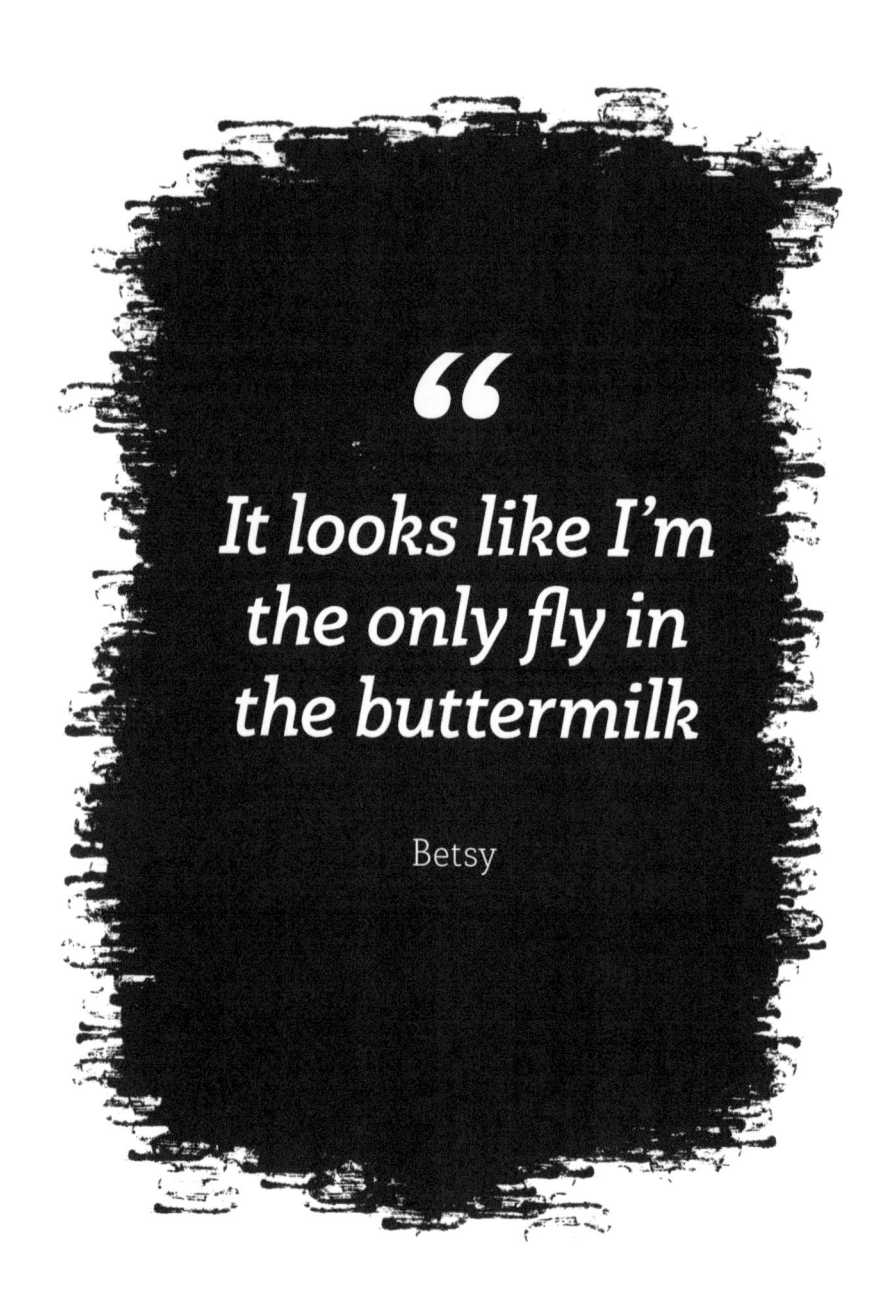

> *It looks like I'm the only fly in the buttermilk*
>
> Betsy

DUALITY OF SIMILARITY

Jamine

Dear White Woman – Ode to you,

I've often reflected on the profound bond we share, one that defies the usual boundaries of difference. You've been my protector, my champion, and my guide. Though the world may see us as two women from different walks of life, I see so much more in you – something deeply familiar, something that feels like home.

I exist because you pushed me beyond our comfort zones, beyond what society expected of us. And in that journey, I've come to see you not just as a White woman, but as an integral part of me. There's something inexplicably familiar in your spirit, something deeply emotional that resonates with my own.

You've never seen me as just another Black woman; you've seen me as someone worthy of support and celebration. Your advocacy has lifted me in ways I can never fully repay. It's almost poetic that our differences, the very things that the world uses to divide us, are what drew us together. In embracing those distinctions, we've found a strength and beauty that defies what the world expects from us.

DEAR WHITE WOMAN, DEAR BLACK WOMAN

The world may look at us through different lenses, but I don't see you through that distorted glass. To me, you are me, and I am you. It's this duality of similarity and difference that I cherish most about our relationship. It's what makes our bond so powerful and unique.

Please, always keep that open mind that has allowed us to grow together. But, never lose that core of you that holds us close, that binds us in solidarity. As you continue to rise and succeed, as I know you will, remember those of us who walk alongside you. I promise to do the same – to uplift and honor our shared journey.

I will cherish you forever, not just for what you've done for me, but for who you are– empathy, understanding, and genuine friendship. Together, we rewrite how the world perceives us and seeks to divide us. Together, we are creating a future where differences are celebrated, not feared.

Thank you for being more than an ally. Thank you for being my sister, my confidant, and my inspiration. Let's continue to defy expectations, break down barriers, and build a world where everyone feels seen and safe.

Let's change the world together,
Jamine

> To me, you are me, and I am you.

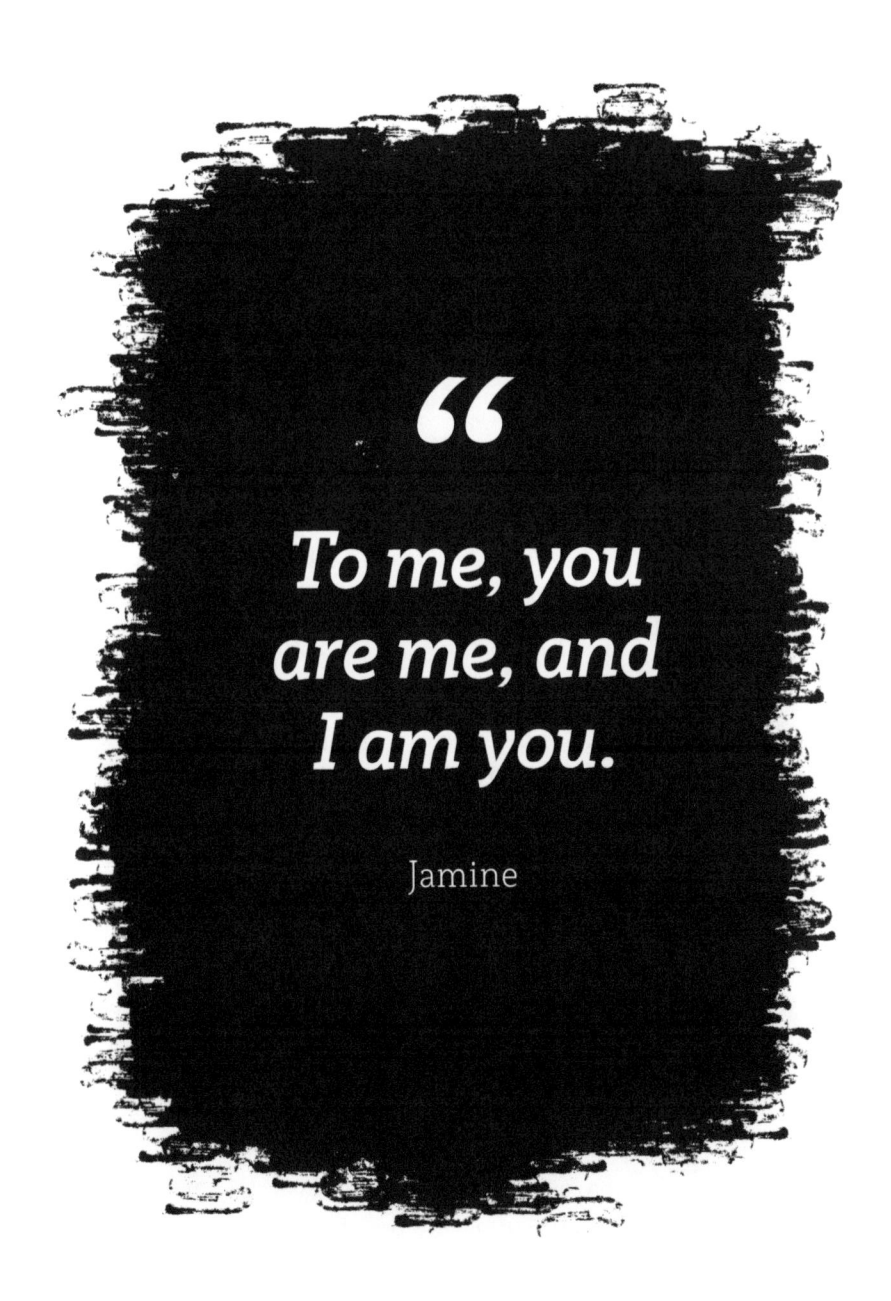

Jamine

MOVING PAST MY ASSUMPTIONS
Maggie

Dear Black Woman,

Writing this letter scares me. Will I say something wrong? Will some unconscious bias that I possess be exposed? Am I virtue signaling by even volunteering to participate? I'm scared of what I may say wrong.

But not really scared. Not the kind of fear that you may feel when you shop at a department store, wondering if the loss protection officer is protecting you or following you to make sure that you aren't shoplifting. I'm not scared like you are when your son has to travel outside of your home enclave, where he is a well-known "good kid," to another area where he might be some young officer's excuse to pull over a Black "boy." I'm not frightened like you must be in so many everyday situations where my skin color protects me.

I'm sorry that I didn't know.

I was raised in Iowa, Western Wisconsin, and Western Michigan. Even in my college bastion of liberal ideals, Ann Arbor, Michigan, there was little exposure to the Black experience; your experience, so I did not learn much about you. When we moved to Atlanta, I thought being colorblind was my goal, but later, far too much later, I learned that this was not enough, not nearly enough.

I'm sorry that I didn't realize.

I chose diverse, public schools for my boys and raised them to be colorblind, but I didn't know that wasn't enough. I raised funds for our public school's foundation so that all children would benefit from the best experience possible, but that, too, was ill-informed. I didn't ask you. I assumed that what your kids needed was the same as what my kids needed. I thought your experience was my experience, just a 'little' harder, maybe.

I had no idea.

Until you could hold it in no longer and you began to tell your stories and share your pain that summer. Oh, that summer! That summer when I tried to explain to my boys why our friends were protesting on the street corners and marching for long withheld justice, then I realized that they, too, did not understand their friends' Black experience could still be harder, even in the "New South."

How did I miss this generational opportunity to educate also?

How did I miss your experience too?

How did I not see it in your eyes before? It was always just below the surface of your beautiful brown, green, hazel eyes – the pain from years of pretending you didn't see the microaggressions and slights. Did I not look you in the eyes? Was I afraid of staring at the pain? Why did we never talk about your experience before that summer? Was it too real or too raw? Did you think I wouldn't care? Did I think it was none of my business? Was it like religion and politics, off limits?

I'm sorry because I do want to know your story and share mine. Mine was hard, too, but not because of my skin color.

I'm very sorry that your life was made harder than mine because you have more melanin in your skin. Still, you are proud of your Black ancestry. I envy that. I am a mutt of Western European nothingness that made my path easier than yours. I wish your path were not made more difficult because of other peoples' ignorance, prejudice, and hate.

I wish I could fix it all today. Still, I have hope for the future.

I rarely heard a racist term in our home growing up, but they were very infrequent. I did not use them so my children did not hear them, and do not, to my knowledge, use them. Therefore, I like to imagine that our grandchildren will be the generation that will finally walk hand-in-hand, being far more than colorblind. Our grandchildren will be truly inclusive.

I'm sorry that I was not a bigger part of the solution earlier.

I didn't know is not a good enough reason.

Can we walk and work together now?

With hope,
Maggie

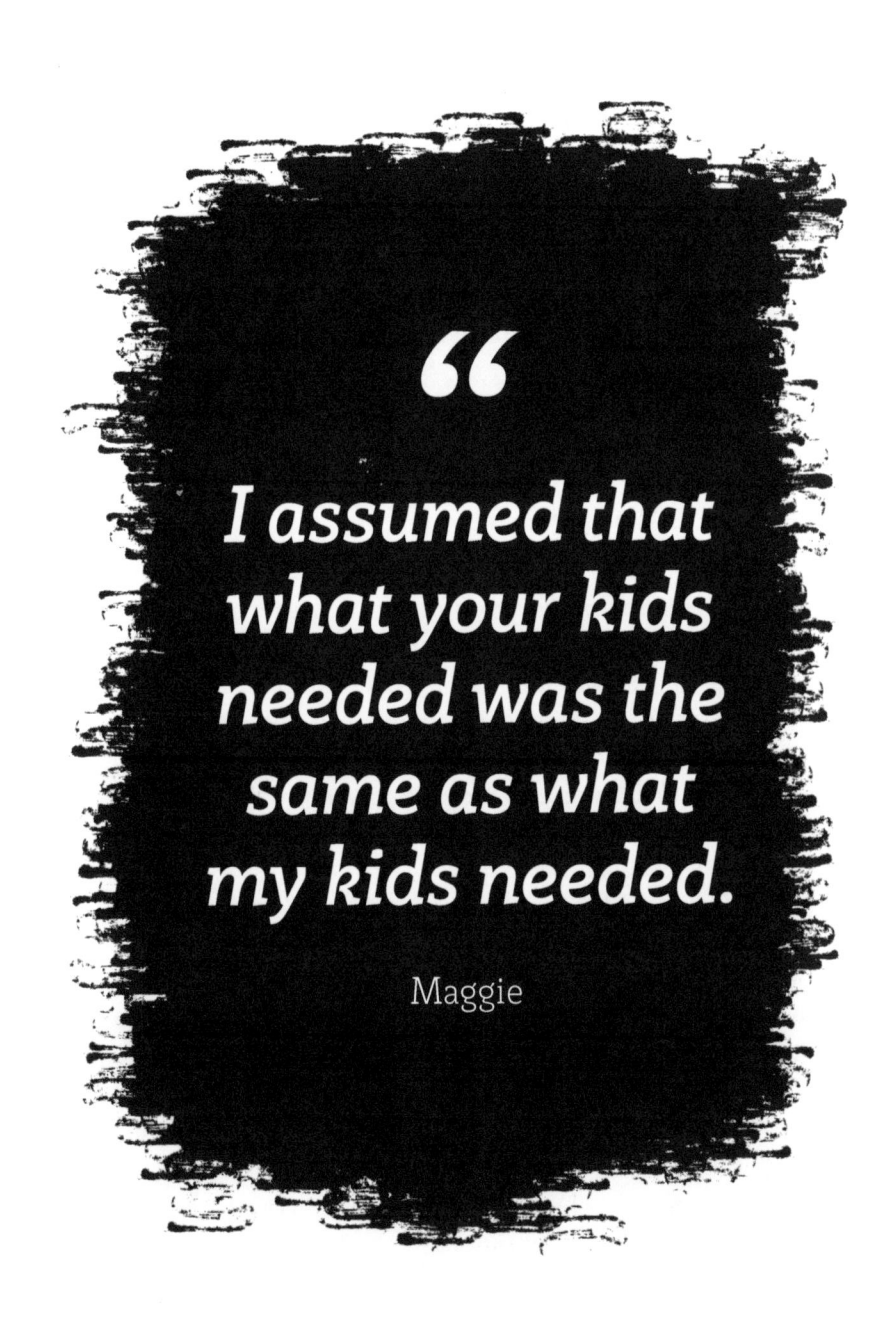

> "I assumed that what your kids needed was the same as what my kids needed.

Maggie

A WORLD MADE JUST FOR YOU

Esther

Dear White Woman,

The world I grew up in looked like a world made just for you. I say that as someone whose first decade was spent in and around a majority-Black Washington, D.C. in the '80s. Other than the everyday presence of my Thai mother, for a time I was surrounded by Black family, neighbors, churchgoers, and schoolmates. So how did I know this time and place called "America" didn't belong to me, in the same way it belonged to you?

Well for starters, Barbie. The line of ubiquitous dolls, which every girl simply had to have, was named for its blonde, blue-eyed star. She was an astronaut. She had a Dreamhouse. She had a commercial jingle that confirmed, "We girls can do anything. Right, Barbie?" Barbie found a Black friend named Christie in the late '60s, and by 1980 Mattel introduced a Black Barbie with a short natural hairstyle. But more frequently, I saw Black Barbies that more or less mimicked OG Barbie's style with long, flowing tresses and a shade of lipstick that didn't quite work with her own deep brown skin tone. My Black Barbie was not the blueprint. She wasn't the center.

Now let's take Hollywood. Women were making strides during my youth. On the big screen, Melanie Griffith found success in a man's world and Diane Keaton dared to become a working mother. Alyssa Milano played the coolest preteen girl on television, and pre-Tiana princesses proliferated. The majority of entertainment centered on white stories, and when I saw a Black main character, it often seemed like being Black was the story. Much like Black history gets a sliver of its due one month a year, role models who resembled me were the exception. Your heroes were the norm.

Another issue you may not have had growing up, experimenting with beauty and learning not to over-pluck your brows, is finding the right foundation. When I came of age, I was no longer living near D.C. but in sunny Florida. It may seem trivial when I say that warm, medium-brown makeup shades were few and far between. Hopping between a few big-box retailers and drug stores, just to find one that even tried to stock a close-enough shade, was not a tragedy. But it was a dismissal. My dollars, my needs, and my preferences were simply not a priority.

I don't begrudge you being seen or being catered to. The fact that protagonists looked more like you, while my skin color matched that of sidekicks and sassy best friends, was just the way of the world. You didn't create it any more than I conjured the stars. But I'd have loved to feel like I belonged. Like I deserved these great United States, which my father's forebears built with their blood, and to which my mother emigrated with dreams in her eyes.

Things have started to change. I've watched it. When commercials stopped insisting exclusively on curly-coiffed, light-skinned, racially ambiguous beauties anytime they cast an African-American woman, I noticed. When Target chose an illustration of a Black couple for their in-store wedding registry, and not specifically for a culture-friendly product line, I was delighted. When Shonda Rhimes built a TV empire where Black characters could be central figures, best friends, bosses, and bad*ss b*tches simply living their drama-filled lives, I celebrated.

Here's what I notice now. I see some of you, seeing me. I see you on Facebook taking no sh*t from either the privileged patriarchy or racist Aunt June. I see you getting full-on academic degrees learning about this construct called race. I see you listening and learning (because if you didn't get that degree, you're likely a bit behind on all of this). I see you standing on a street, holding a sign that says "Black Lives Matter." Because of all the things that shouldn't have to be said, this one really and truly must be affirmed, with every voice, at the top of our lungs.

Dear White Woman, don't stop. Keep being an ally and let's create the America we deserve.

Because in this nation, in this land that was made for you and me, we girls… Can. Do. Anything.

With belief,
Esther

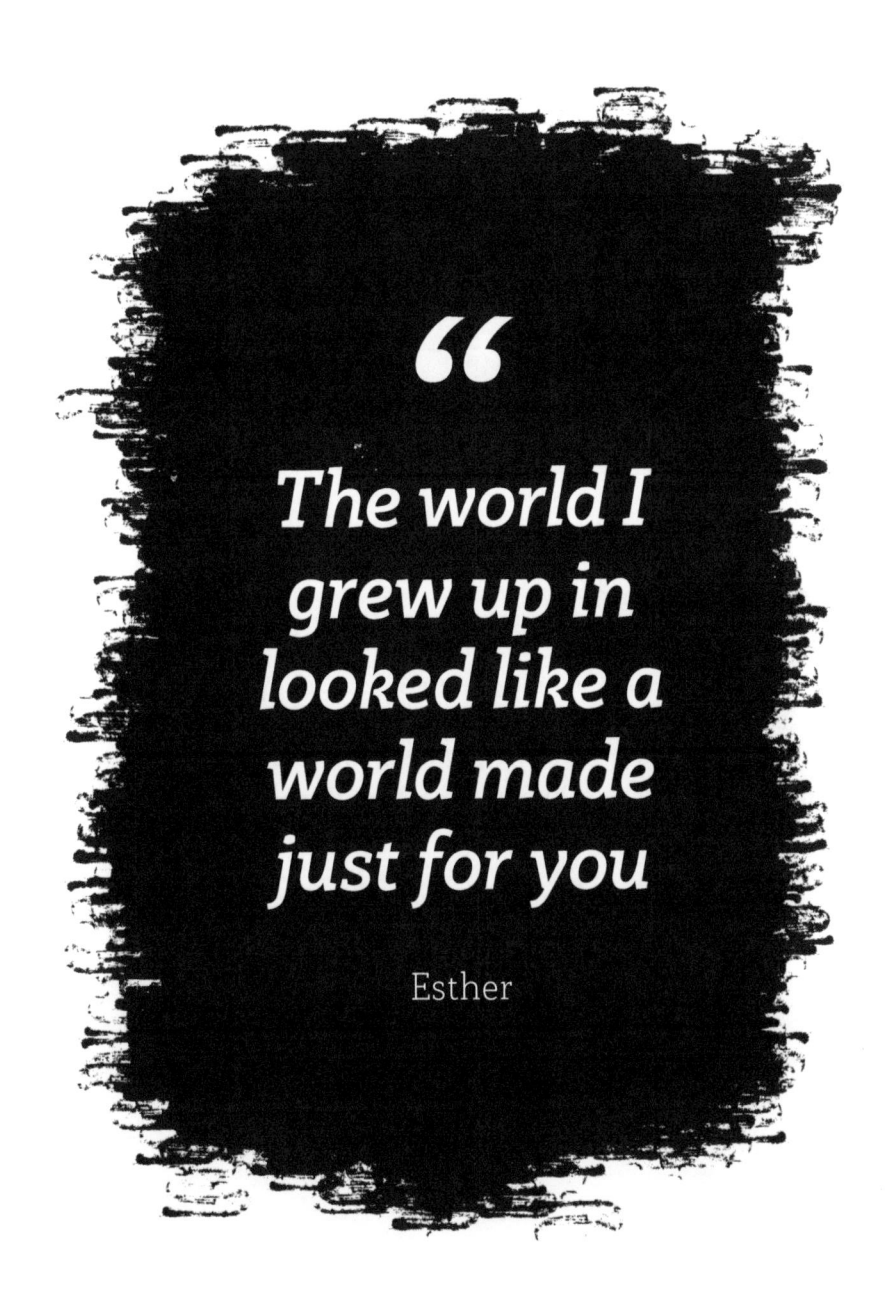

> **The world I grew up in looked like a world made just for you**
>
> Esther

SEEING MYSELF AS SOMEONE LOVEABLE

Anonymous

Dear Black Woman,

Until recently, I thought I was free of prejudice regarding race. The history of my relationship with Black people goes like this: I grew up in Dorchester, Mass. My parents would call Black people "schvartze" which in Yiddish meant black; however, I took it as offensive, and **it was meant that way.** I didn't like it. We moved when I was ten, to a White, Jewish middle-class neighborhood. I remember my folks saying that the schvarzes were moving in . . . time to go!

A more in-depth relationship with a Black person came when I was sixteen, working for the summer at a resort on Cape Cod. While there, I became friends with Jamil, a Haitian artist by day, and a janitor at night. I admired him, and did not think about his circumstances, or why he was a janitor at night.

As a social worker, my first job was with DFCS (Department of Family and Children's Services) in Oakland, California All of my clients were Black. They were kind and protective toward me;

however, what was most important to me was that they valued me, and that I mattered to them. I believed I was ok because of how they saw me. I was unaware, at the time, that my clients were helping me to see myself as someone lovable.

For a long time, I wanted to be Black until I read *Black Like Me*, and decided it was too scary because of the dye Griffin used that ultimately killed him. My desire to be Black had been long-standing. Although I wanted to be Black, I did not think about the discrimination that came along with skin color. Or that somewhere inside me, I felt like I was "better than" Black people.

Racism was on the periphery of my awareness, even after reading *Waking Up White* several years ago. What struck me about the book was that a White woman, who thought she was liberal, came to realize that she was quietly prejudiced. Although I loved the book, and thought it should be required reading for all White people, reading it did not change me – not really.

I connected with Black people: raised a child that was Black, had good friends and lovers that were Black, and worked with a Black staff and Black grandparents raising grandchildren. And, yet I was still kidding myself about what it meant to be Black in America.

As immersed as I was in Black culture, I had not taken the time to learn about what was happening in my country around race, and my particular brand of racism. I paid no real attention to discrimination, until the George Floyd murder and the Black Lives Matter movement.

I have been horrified at what has come to light around race, and at the same time, I am learning about my own prejudice.

For example, I bought a doll that sang "Respect" by Aretha Franklin; she moved her head like Black women often do, **and** she looked like a monkey! I remember when I bought it, I thought it was funny. I **did not** notice that the doll was a monkey. I showed it to my Black friends, and whatever they may have felt, they did not say anything to me about the inherent racism of the doll.

Where I am now . . . I am conscious of my subtle attitudes of racism. I am disheartened by the prejudice I see around me, and hopeful that a long overdue change is coming, especially because the next generation, that has grown up in a diverse world, sees color as a non-issue.

Finally, I am thankful that race is at the forefront now. I recognize that I have grown up in a racist society, which means that I am inherently racist. Therefore to change, I need to be conscious of how racism is present in my life. Since my awareness of racial inequities, I am conscious of how my thoughts and feelings around race create my own form of racism, no matter how innocent it appears to me.

With thanks,
A White Woman Who Now Sees

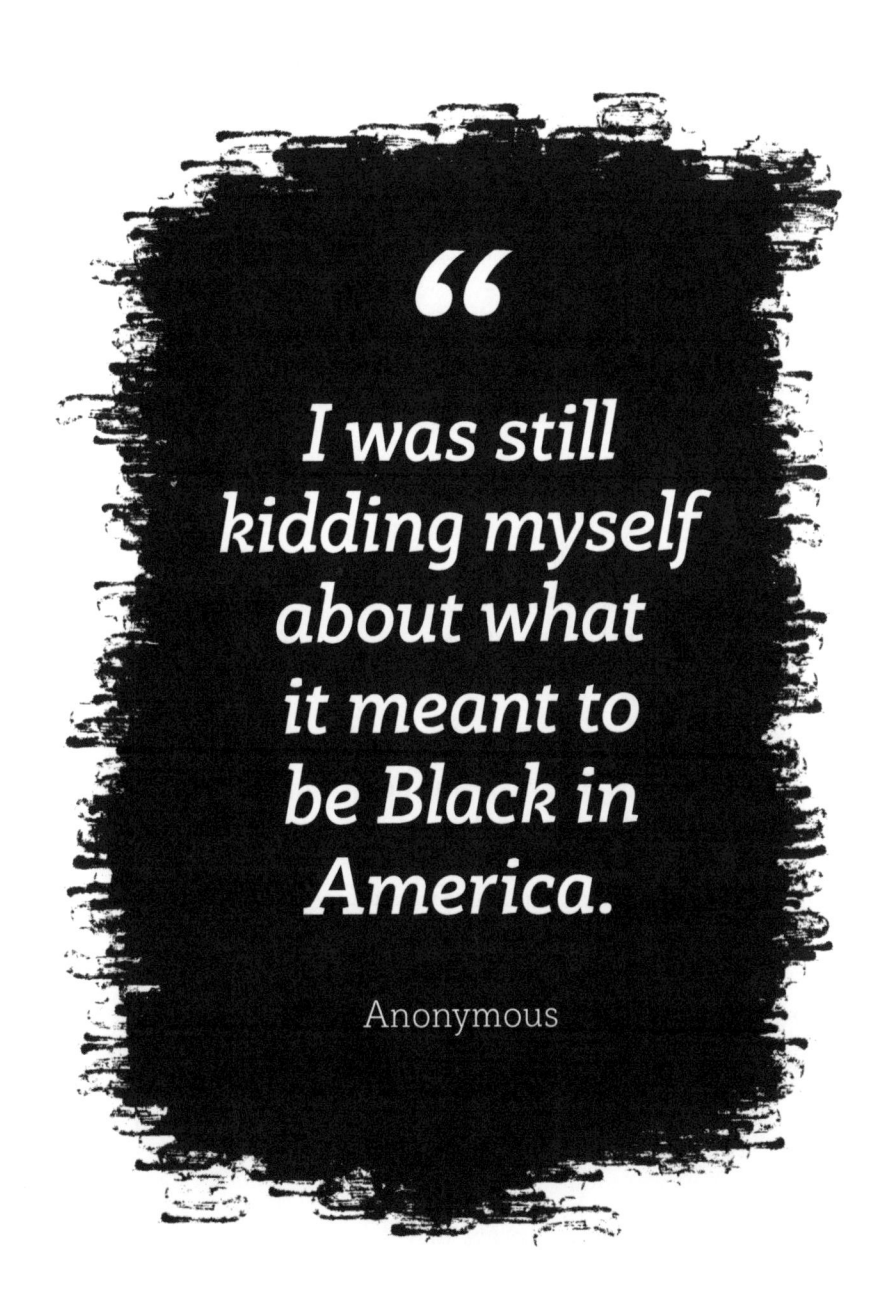

> *I was still kidding myself about what it meant to be Black in America.*

Anonymous

DON'T FEAR MY BROTHER

Jacqueline

Dear White Woman,

I am polite to you, just like I am polite to all the strangers I meet on the street. I say good morning to them just like I say good morning to people I know. So, you should not fear me or anyone who shares my skin or my natural hair texture.

If you don't fear me, don't fear my brother. He wears a hoodie because he's cold. He moves with angst because he's usually accused and ostracized. Don't accuse falsely, cross the street when he approaches, call the law when he knocks on your door, or clutch your purse as he enters the elevator.

He doesn't come to steal and kill, neither do I. We don't have the power to do so. You are really in control of the world you live in. We move back to allow you to pass because we know you command respect, we listen when you speak even though our ears decipher what we hear, and we smile with glee when our paychecks signed by you are cleared for cash.

Whether you took this world by force or it was given to you, it's yours through systemic racism and that's not going away or easing up without your intentional response. To have a more trusting society where we decide to live together in peace, I need you not to vilify us at the dinner table. I need you not to point us out as a thief because we're jogging, not running away. I need you not to see a monkey at the zoo and refer to it as your Black housekeeper or co-worker in the presence of your child. I need you to not identify us as the culprit because we look like the assailant but he was six feet with tan eyes and curly black hair, and I am five feet with black eyes and curly nappy black hair.

If you would view us as people and not animals, the rest of the world would also, and most importantly, your children would and they wouldn't grow up to think they're better in any way. They wouldn't project upon the world, notably the United States, that they are privileged and therefore, have every right to attack the capitol or to choke a man to death with cameras rolling without consequence. They also will not subconsciously expect to lead without skills or deny a person of color the chance to lead. They will expect to be treated equally and treat others equally as well.

It starts and ends with you White Woman.

Politely,
Jacqueline

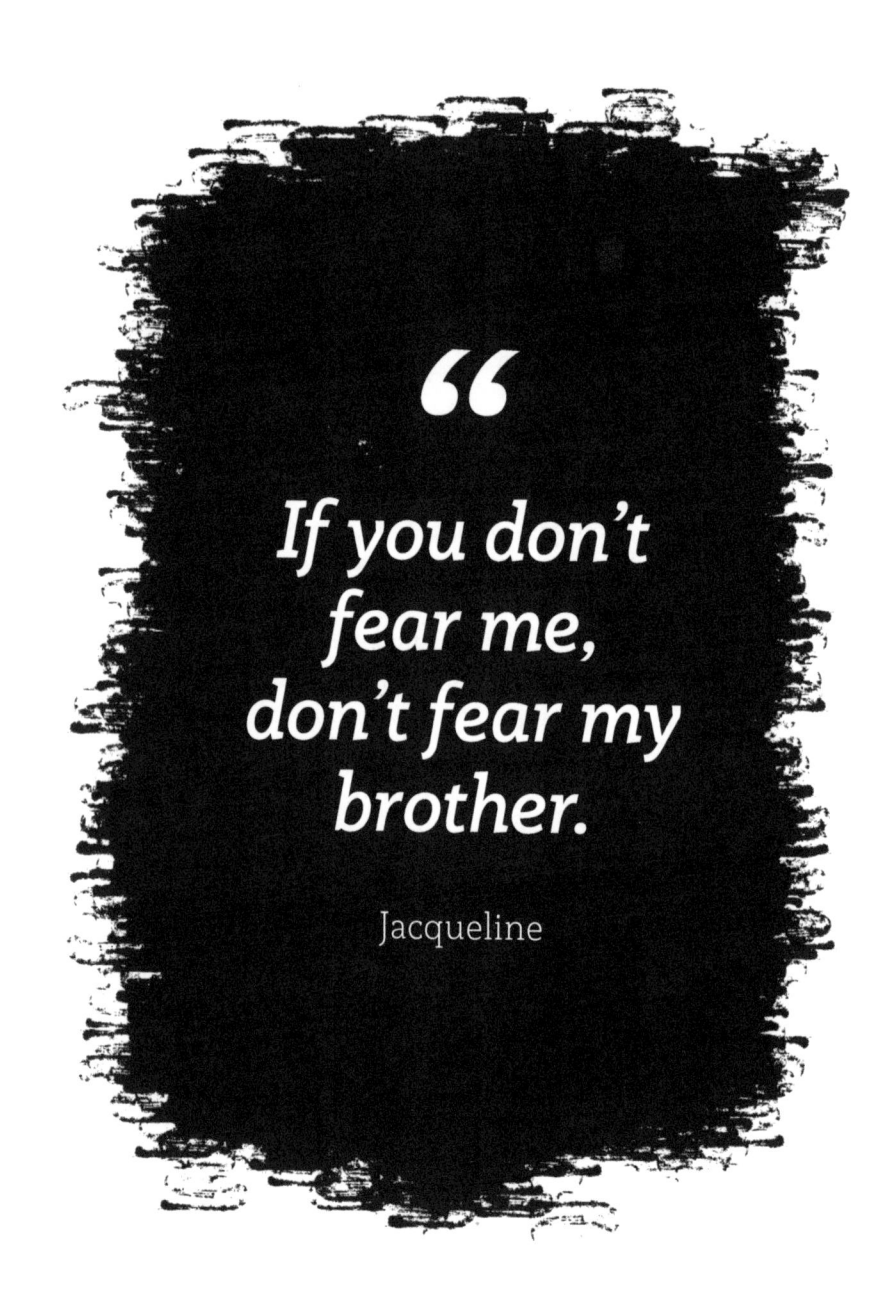

> **If you don't fear me, don't fear my brother.**
>
> Jacqueline

UNWORTHY

Abby

Dear Black Woman,

Writing this letter has been one of the hardest things I have ever done in my life. I have a million things I want to say, and none of them feel worthy.

I am sitting here thinking of how I will never understand the struggles you face every day. The judgments that are passed the minute you enter a room before you have even said a word. The biases you face from a world living in fear and insecurity, rarely questioning the source or the historical significance.

I am **angry** at my ancestors for creating arbitrary legislation and verbiage to create separation amongst humans: especially around women and Black women. I am **afraid** that White people will give up the fight when it's not the "cool" thing to do or the media is quiet. I **worry** that we will stop questioning each other and educating ourselves and being vulnerable in the discomfort of not knowing. I am sad that people would rather go along with the status quo than be vulnerable, question everything, and make ripples.

My heart is filled with **empathy** for the struggles you face every day. Since I was a child, I have been surrounded by the most amazing, strong, and courageous women of color – and I have not always known the struggles they were facing. Each of them has shown me through their actions a beautiful, bright, and inclusive world.

I don't know your story, but I want to know. I know that my privilege has allowed me to move in the world differently. I want to use that to listen and to continue questioning everything and inviting everyone I know to have hard conversations – to plant seeds for future generations, to celebrate representation, to be vulnerable, and to create a world where we stay curious and move forward together.

I am grateful for you. Your bad*ssery. Your resilience in a world that doesn't consistently advocate for you. Thank you for being and for showing up every day – you are so loved.

Sincerely,
Abby

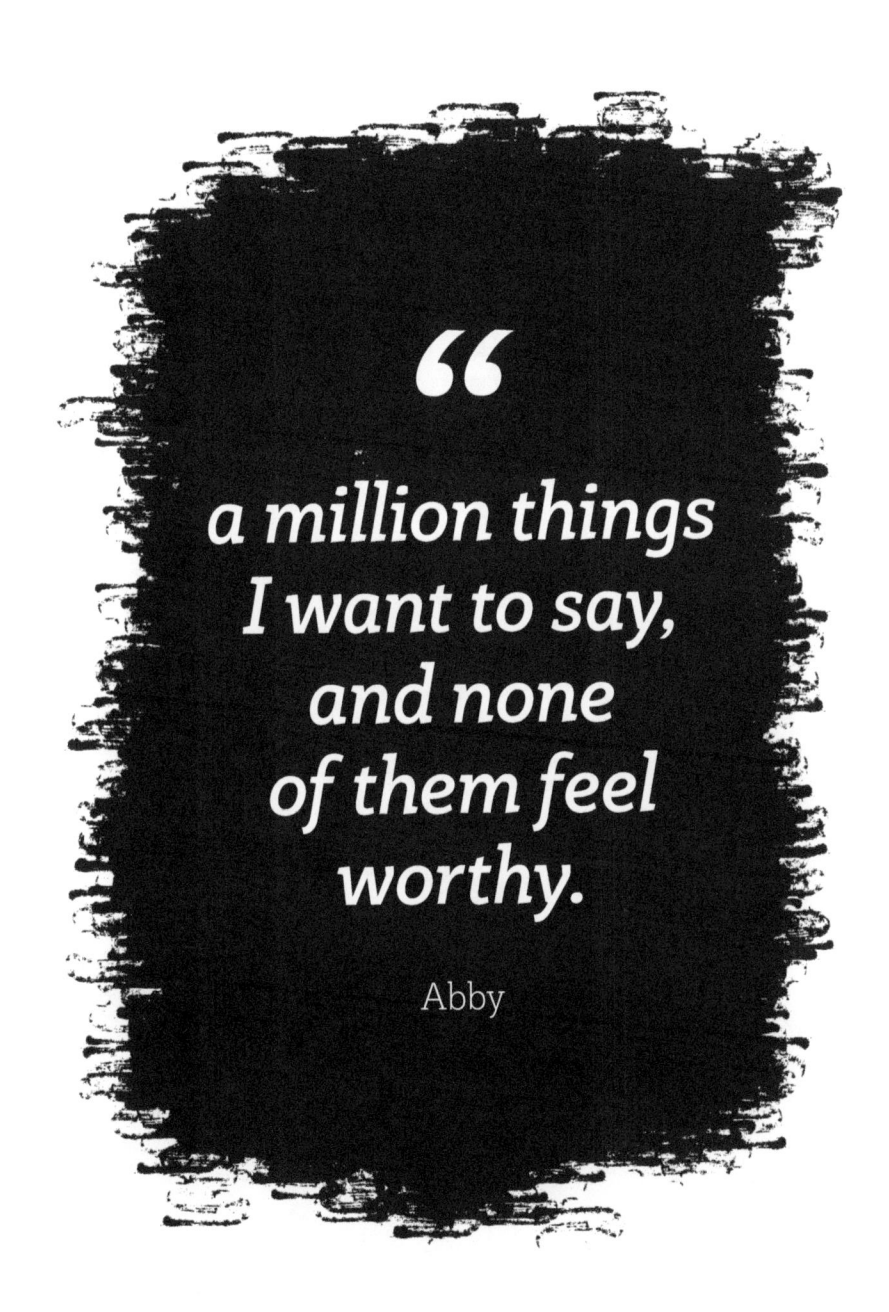

> *a million things I want to say, and none of them feel worthy.*
>
> Abby

TO WHITE WOMEN IN CORPORATE AMERICA

Anonymous

Dear White Woman,

Do you know how much your co-workers need you? Do you know how much your voice matters in this space? Do you know you can change my career trajectory with your advocacy? Do you know we're more alike than we are different?

Have you ever been the only person in a room that looked like you? Have you ever gotten dressed for work and thought your professionalism may be questioned? Have you ever not spoken up during a meeting or conversation because you don't want to seem too boisterous? Have you ever had to second-guess yourself because you don't want to seem too emotional, or in some situations, too nonchalant? Have you ever not wanted to come into the office because you just got your hair done and you don't want to be judged, or for your hair to be discussed, or even touched?

Have you ever had someone mispronounce your name, and you are scared to correct them because you don't want to intimidate them? Have you ever been asked why you don't participate in after-hours events? Do you know that I'm fighting a battle against patriarchy and unconscious bias?

The world as we know it has changed, but together, we can ensure it changes for the better. I want you to know that we are allies in this fight for social and racial justice. It's not about me, it's about us, it's about our daughters, and our granddaughters. It's time for us to learn more about each other so that we can fight the powers that are working against us. It's time for us to realize that we are interconnected, and when my life changes for the better, so does yours. It's time for us to put our differences aside, listen to each other, and make tangible, long-lasting, and impactful change.

This memorandum is to help you understand what I go through, sometimes on a daily basis. It is my hope that you will not take it as a personal attack but as a personal opportunity to understand what it's truly like to be a Black woman in America – specifically in corporate spaces. It's not as easy as we make it look, but we make it look damn good! So take this as your chance to say, the change starts with me, and the cycle ends with me.

Just think of the stories you'll be able to tell your children, and their children, about how you helped changed the world. How you helped create more inclusive and equitable opportunities for all people. How you helped the world be closer to what God created it to be.

The choice is yours; what are you going to do?

We appreciate you,
A Black Woman with a Lot to Lose

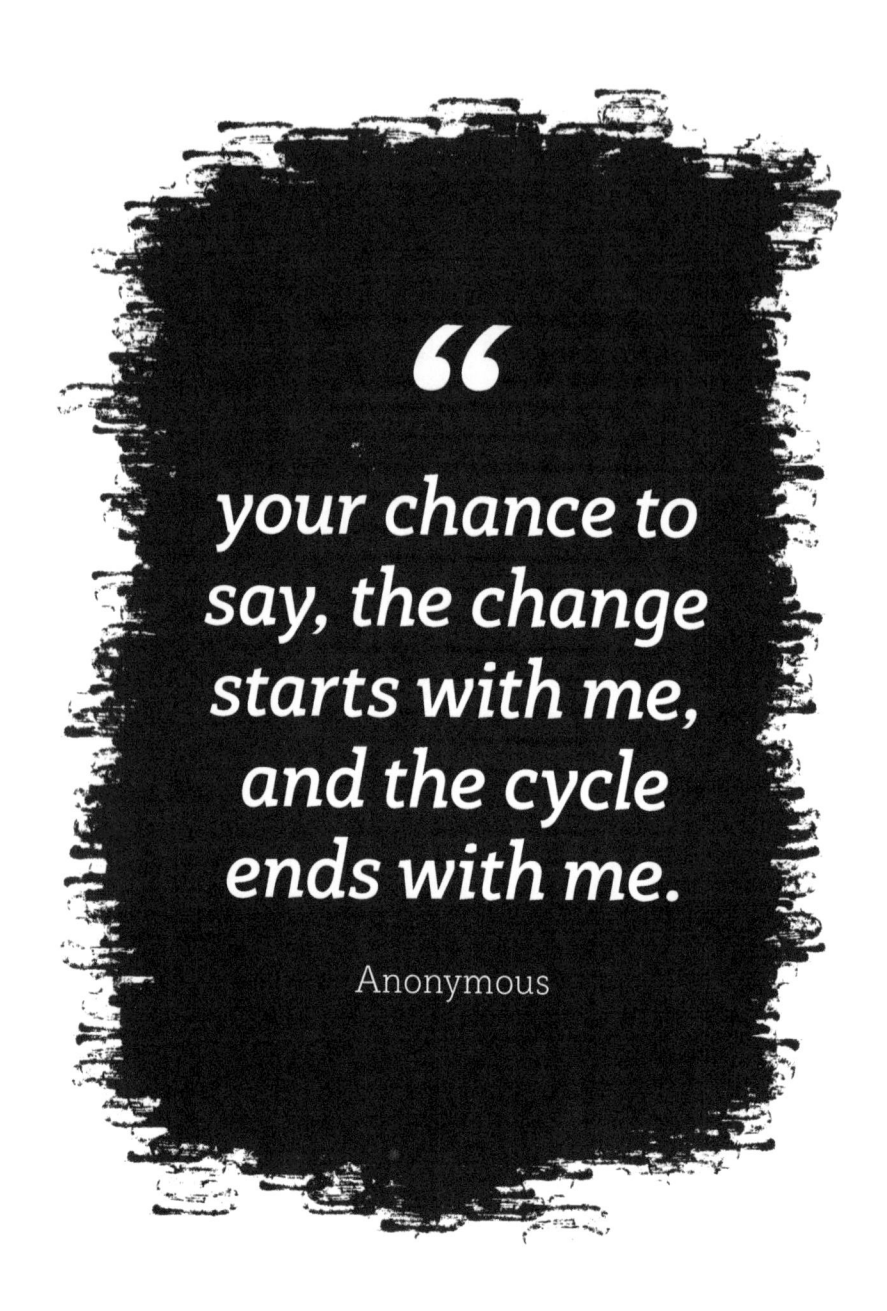

> "your chance to say, the change starts with me, and the cycle ends with me.

Anonymous

MOVING BEYOND APOLOGIES

Stacy

Dear Black Woman,

I am so sorry.

I'm sorry that you live in a racist society and culture.

I'm sorry that this means that you're likely to have a lower income, less accumulated wealth, higher maternal mortality, and all the other ugly statistics when you're compared to other demographics.

I'm sorry that you have to work harder and be better than your White counterparts, and that even this doesn't guarantee equal treatment.

I'm sorry that you can't show the anger that you must certainly feel.

I'm sorry that our country relies on you to vote blue, and without you, we would have far fewer progressive politicians protecting us.

I'm sorry that I didn't truly understand the impact of systemic racism until George Floyd was murdered, and I finally read all the books and had the difficult conversations.

I'm sorry that I didn't understand that my version of feminism doesn't help you much. Again, I've done reading and research and now understand how critical intersectionality is in feminism, as it is with all things.

I'm sorry that I didn't know what microaggressions are until I faced them working in a misogynistic company (and even then, it's probably nothing compared with what you deal with every day).

I'm sorry that your mother may have taught you to only bring a small clutch bag into stores so you couldn't be accused of shoplifting, as one of my daughter's friends was taught (and my daughter was not).

I'm sorry that when someone on Facebook asked, "When's the first time a cop pointed a gun at you?" that you had an answer for that and I didn't.

I'm sorry that my friends and I have relied on you to teach us what it's like to be Black in America, not realizing that this both "others" you from the group and has a larger emotional impact on you than us.

I'm sorry that I never joined a "Black Lives Matter" protest until 2020.

I'm sorry that I am virtue signaling in this very letter because I so desperately want to separate myself from "them."

You deserve better. You have always deserved better. There is no one stronger and more beautiful on this planet than you. I am sorry that not everyone sees it ... yet. I see it. I see you. And collectively, I hope we can do better so that your daughters and granddaughters won't need all these apologies.

With love,
Stacy
Atlanta, Georgia

> *so that your daughters and granddaughters won't need all these apologies*
>
> Stacy

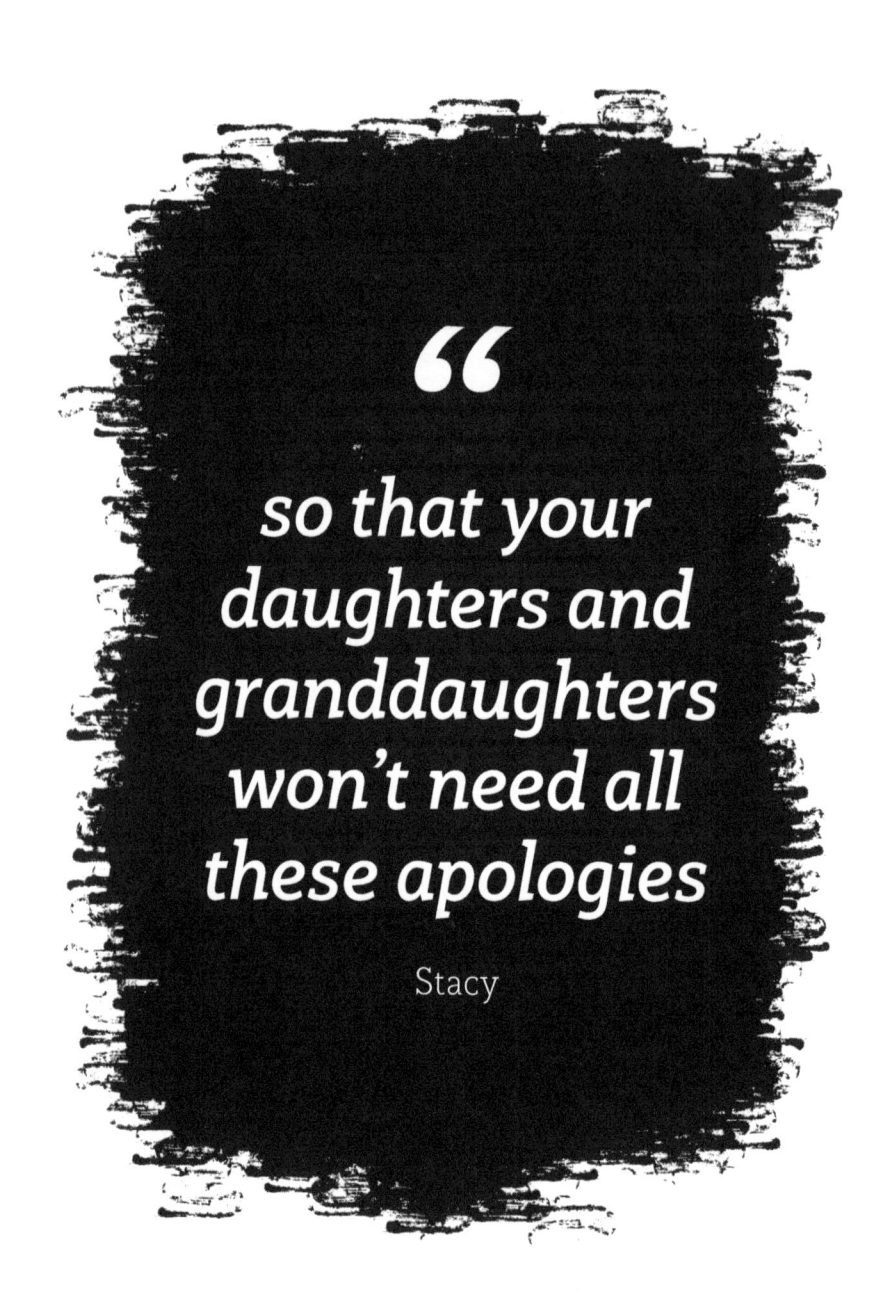

SIS

Anonymous

Dear White Woman, Sis. . .

Please describe for me the texture of our culture, that you slip over your head and down around your ankles side of the bed at your convenience. Like a one night stand. . .sis. . .you didn't call us in the morning, after the march on Washington, we walked, ran, flew back to our respectful places, to be with familiar faces and pretended we believed that this was about equality and damned be division between the races. Because Irreverence drowns the phantom moaning of our hollow wombs, tombs that arrest the memories of the Relisha Rudds.

But sis, I bet when you were at the supermarket, buying your arts and crafts at Target to carefully construct your pussy hats, you'll still see Jon Bennet Ramsey immortalized on the news racks. A white child whose story we never stopped chasing. While time past seems to be erasing the brown bodies picked off the street, like the ripest of the strange fruit hanging from the poplar tree.

My sister, at the intersection of race and gender, is the Black woman. They built yo' land on my back woman, the angry woman, the hard woman, they pull rabbits out my ass with no applause woman. Do the work two times over for my seat at the table woman. The able woman. Because "I have to" woman. The "I wore my pussy hat too" woman. . . I stood with y'all when my heart wasn't all the way in it, like eff it, let's end it, we are women before color.

However, as a woman of color, it is deeply offensive that while Black women are magic y'all know we ain't orchestrating this disappearing act. So, where the hashtags at? Where are the rally cries for this genocide? For all the missing brown bodies in your nation's capital, where they're trafficking for capital, they pillage and plunder, in hoods where we hunger, mamas working two jobs so bills don't go under. And fathers are under, the foot or the bars of the man, the way of the land. . . so when babies go missing. . .ain't nobody listening. . .they call'em runaways.

But sis, I know y'all ain't know that. Because that's not your reality. But what's real for me. . .is our kids going to the piss po'ist schools, playing by your rules. And still someone's mother is crying tears of loss and unknowing. My womb is not growing, targets for police and meat for pedophiles. Blue files, stacked on the desk of the district, the names of our missing, reduced to numbers and incidents.

Ay sis, you don't like me like you say you do. I'm out here stamping and chanting about some sh*t that felt good in the moment, freeze it, and hold it. This pseudo closeness. But not quite close enough to feel this juxtaposition; our children are missing.

So. . . all my privileged ladies. . . put ya hands up!
Sis, can ya hear me now?
Sis, can you see me now?
Sister, can you feel me now?
Fight with me. Fight for me. Find our girls.

– Anonymous

> *Ay sis, you don't like me like you say you do.*

Anonymous

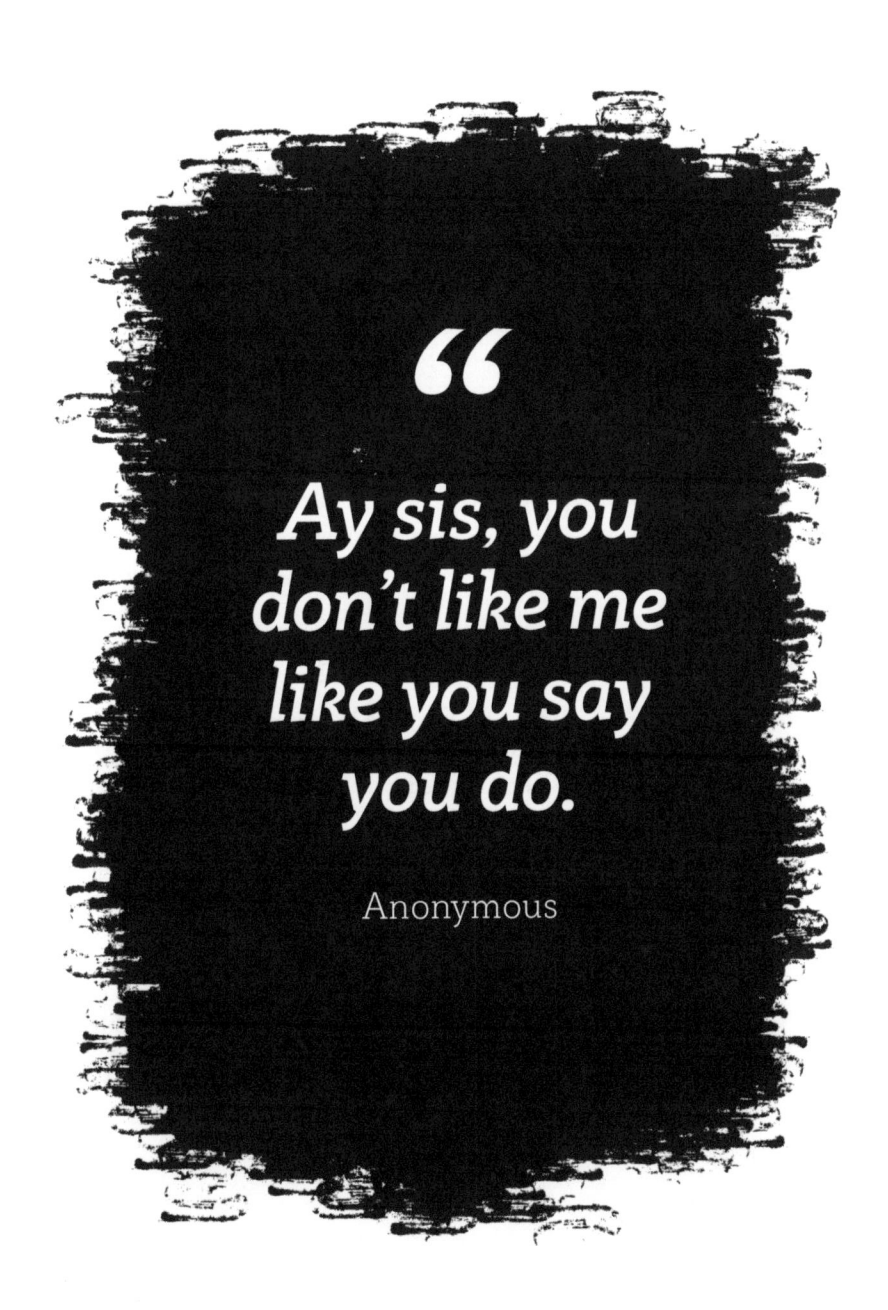

HEAD OF THE TABLE

Ashley

Dear Black Woman,

You are loved.

I am so sorry the world, myself included, has not done a good job of showing you this. You are created so beautifully as a Black woman, and yet, throughout the history of the United States, you have been feared, mistreated, used, and abused. Your intricate and deep complexities are simplified down to pigment for someone else's benefit. Because of the darkness of your skin and the texture of your hair, you are identified as "other," which can also translate to "less than." You, of course, are not "less than" – but I know it takes so much effort not to believe that when that's how you're treated day after day, year after year.

You are beautiful.
You are worthy.
You are good.
You are powerful.

Not because I say so, but because it's how you were created by God. You are a glorious human being.

My heart hurts to think of how long you've been asking us to open our eyes and do something about the injustices you've suffered. Even the White churches have failed, teaching from a narrative of Whiteness and separation, when the truth comes from a Brown Jesus with a heart of inclusion and radical love.

Our education and media are Whitewashed, and you've been gaslit for so long. Jim Crow was not that long ago and racism is still very real... Our own fears and insecurities have held us back from truly loving you, our sister, and I am sorry.

Our White generation is waking up to your Black realities and we see you. We see the fear of letting your loved ones leave your house. We see the disparities in medical care. We see the fear of raising your children in a White-centered America. We see your voice dismissed, your truth ignored. We see the fear of cops and we are starting to understand. We are sorry.

But apologies aren't enough. Actions speak louder than words and we are learning to choose love over fear.

You have allies. We are growing in numbers. The road ahead is still going to be rough. There is still White supremacy that runs deep and it's ugly. But you don't have to fight alone. We are joining you in the marches to lock arms and stand with you. We are learning to pass the mic and give you the platform you need and deserve. We want to hear your voice. We want to know your story. We want to see your freedom and success and watch you soar. Will you forgive us?

I call on my White brothers and sisters right now, in this moment: If you wondered what you would've done when Martin Luther King Jr. was alive, what are you doing now? The fight is ongoing and his heart for equity is still beating strong. It looks a little different than it did back then, but the calling is still here. This moment. Right now. How will you answer? What do you stand for?

Our Black brothers and sisters have been fighting and they're tired. Let's join together and give them rest. Let's build a better America for them and for our children. Let's answer the call.

Some of the ways I am learning to answer is to speak up against injustices. Call the D.A.'s office and other government officials to petition and call for justice when there's been a wrong. Read books by Black authors. Learn the full history and be open to new narratives that challenge my own. Vote intentionally. Spend money purposefully with Black businesses. Have the hard conversations. Support Black youth and create new opportunities for them. Check our White privilege and our hearts. We have all been taught racism, and it's our responsibility as White people in a system that works for us to do the anti-racist work.

I know the world will never be perfect. It's in life's struggles that we learn and grow. But let our struggles not be struggles of hate. Let us not allow fear to take control. Let us not war against each other. Let ours be struggles of learning to rest and try again. Let ours be struggles of relationship-building, deepening our understanding of ourselves and our community. We are richer in our differences. Let us work together to save the earth from the current trajectory we are on. *That* is a worthy struggle.

Dear Black Woman – I hope you feel the support coming. It's been too long. I imagine your heart is weary and you're tired. I see you have no choice but to keep fighting to survive. Help is coming. Systems won't change as quickly as you need them to, and it may take longer than we hope for, but relief is on the horizon. Women are joining together in the divine feminine to bring balance, love, and healing to you and to the world. I hope you feel it.

Dear Black Woman, I am with you. I am **for** you.

I see a world in the not-so-distant future where you can have peace. Where you can kiss your son as he walks out the door and not have fear in your heart that he may not come home alive. A world where we can be neighbors without any second thoughts or red lines. I see a new reality where you are safe. Where Black Lives Matter and racist cops are brought to justice. Where officers of the law work to protect you from harm and are trauma-informed to diffuse intense situations without weapons. A world where all women would be guaranteed equal opportunities and equal pay to pursue the life we have dreamed of . . . where you can be the head of the table instead of fighting for a seat at it. Where you can have unapologetic joy. Where your kids can be anything they want to be.

Dear Black Woman, you're not alone.

You are loved,
Ashley

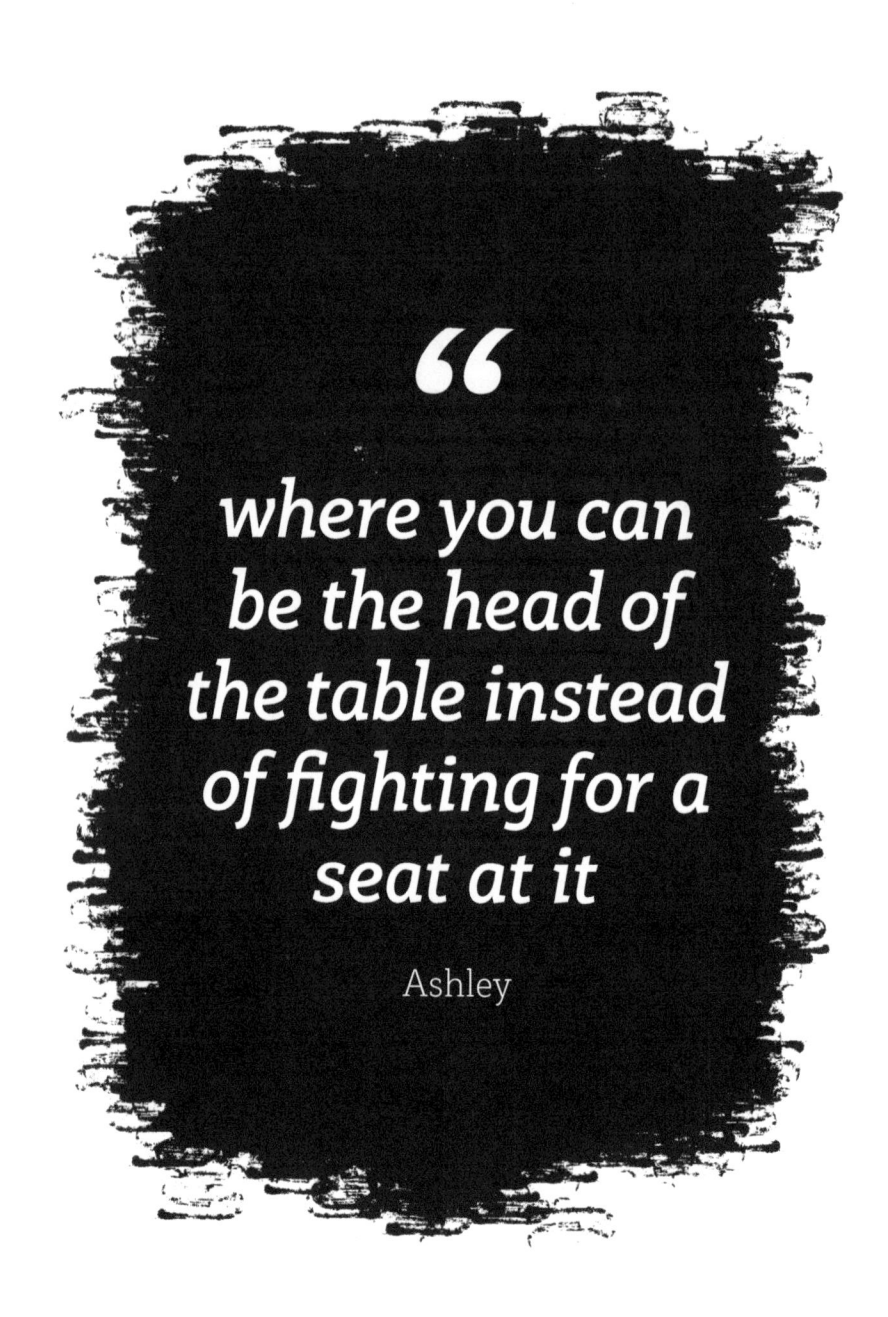

> "where you can be the head of the table instead of fighting for a seat at it
>
> Ashley

DESERVING RESPECT

Lori

Dear White Woman,

I am all that and more, why? Because I earned every right to be where I am. A strong Black woman, an amazing Educator, and a marvelous mother. I worked 100 times harder than you to get the respect that I earned and deserve. Yes, I walk with my head held high and my shoulders straight back because I'm proud of who I am and where I came from. Growing up, we weren't rich with money, but we were rich with love, kindness, and strength. My parents wanted the best for us, so they sacrificed and worked many jobs to make sure we received the best education.

I became an inner-city teacher so that I can continue to spread love, kindness, and strength to children who look like me and to let them know how beautiful and important they are to this world.

You say I think I'm all that because I'm the only Black teacher in the school. I was truly insulted that those words could come out of your mouth, especially in front of students. You should be ashamed of yourself. Well, dear White woman. . . I am all that and more because I **am** an intelligent, strong, and phenomenal Black woman.

DEAR WHITE WOMAN, DEAR BLACK WOMAN

Don't apologize for your ignorance, do something to prove that you've learned something from your experience with me... but dear White woman, I forgive you.

Sincerely,
Lori
Windsor, Connecticut

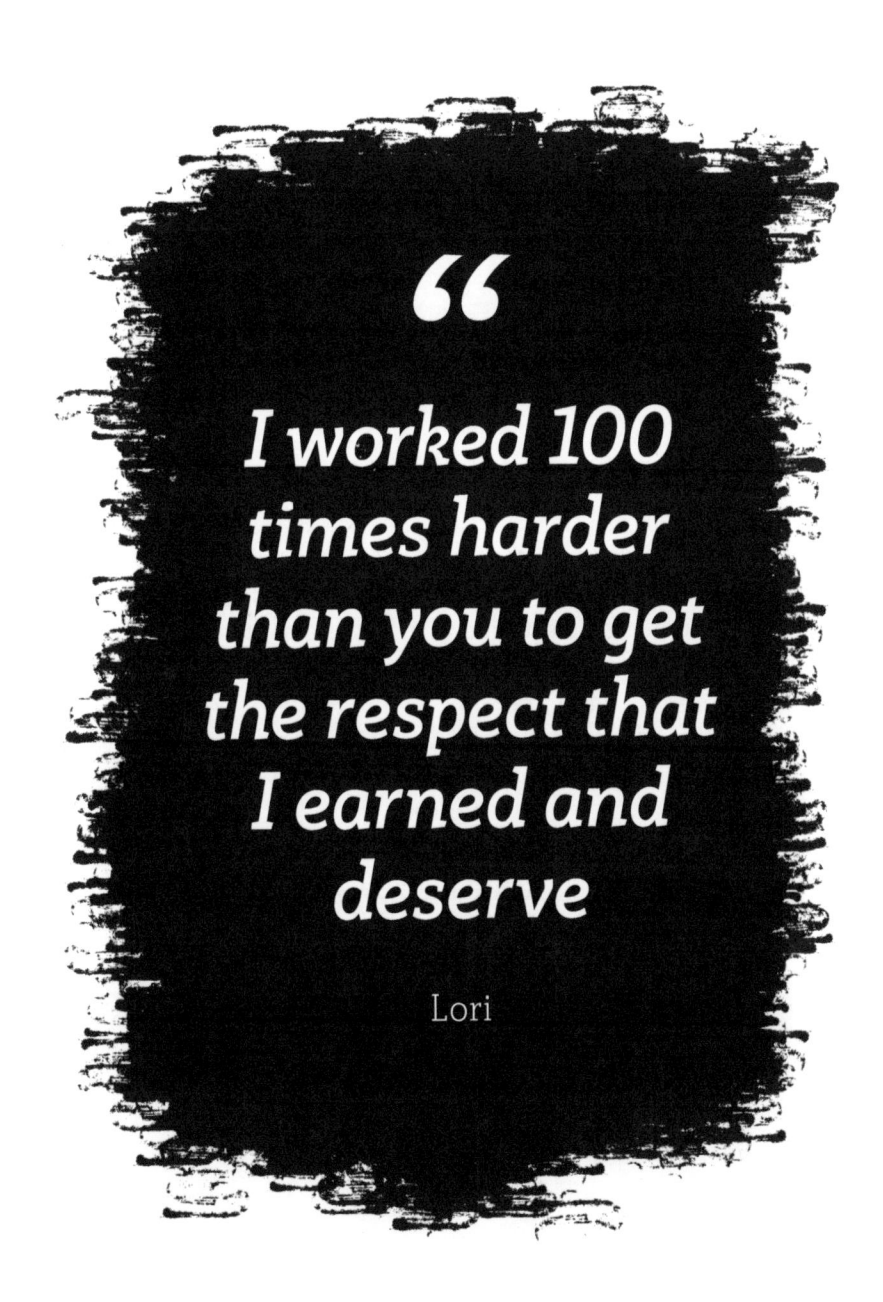

> "I worked 100 times harder than you to get the respect that I earned and deserve

Lori

LIGHTING THE WAY

Anonymous

Dear Black Woman,

I'm sorry. Please forgive me. Thank you. I love you. These words are from the Hawaiian healing prayer Ho'oponopono. A friend from France once shared this with me and these words have stuck with me ever since. Said together, they have a way of setting us free.

I'm sorry.

I'm sorry for the heavy burden you've carried that was not yours in the first place. I'm sorry for being asleep to this for so long, for not questioning my privilege sooner. I'm sorry for not stopping to feel your pain and to listen to your story more carefully. I'm sorry my empathy did not break through the sound barrier of my privilege to shake me from my slumber. I'm sorry it took me nearly forty years of walking this Earth to stop and get uncomfortable. I'm sorry for how many White women out there are choosing to go back to sleep. I'm sorry I didn't stand beside you sooner.

Please forgive me.

Please forgive me for choosing comfort, for I did not examine at whose expense it came. Please forgive me for dismissing the whispers of my intuition at the country club or the private party, *this isn't right*. Please forgive me for thinking these were the way things were and that I couldn't do anything about them. Please forgive me for not speaking up louder or sooner when I witnessed microaggressions. Please forgive me for my blindness and compliance to the white culture as it stifled and threatened you. Please forgive me for thinking I understood more than I did as a half-Jew with unwelcomed Jewish jokes from non-Jewish friends growing up. Please forgive me for not taking the time earlier to sit with your stories and to get to know you better.

Thank you.

Thank you for your soul. Thank you for your perseverance and your wisdom. Thank you for all the beauty you bring into the world and for the ease with which it flows when you share it. Thank you for your grace and beauty despite whatever you are facing. Thank you for modeling true feminine power, in your strength and humble presence. Thank you for knowing and trusting yourself and for opening the door to me. Thank you for your patience. Thank you for trusting me and taking the time as I stumble. Thank you for teaching me and showing me and creating brave space to explore together. Thank you for your creativity, your passion, your inspiration, and your spark. You light up the darkness with your presence.

I love you.

I love you Black Woman. I love you like a sister. When I let you in and let my guard down, I found you were my sister. My closest friend during dark and lonely times, a steady presence for all who need you. I love you, friend. I love you more and more, with every day I get to know you. I am humbled by your story and the strength you carry. I love the incredible human you are. I love the light you bring to the darkness. I love the essence of your being. I love all that you inspire.

Keep shining bright dear sister. Shine bright. Don't let our fragile selves misguide you. We are learning and we are watching, and we are waking as we do. Your presence lights the way, inspiring us on the way to better. Your magic and your presence inspire us to be more like you.

Love,
Anonymous White Woman

> "Your presence lights the way, inspiring us on the way to better

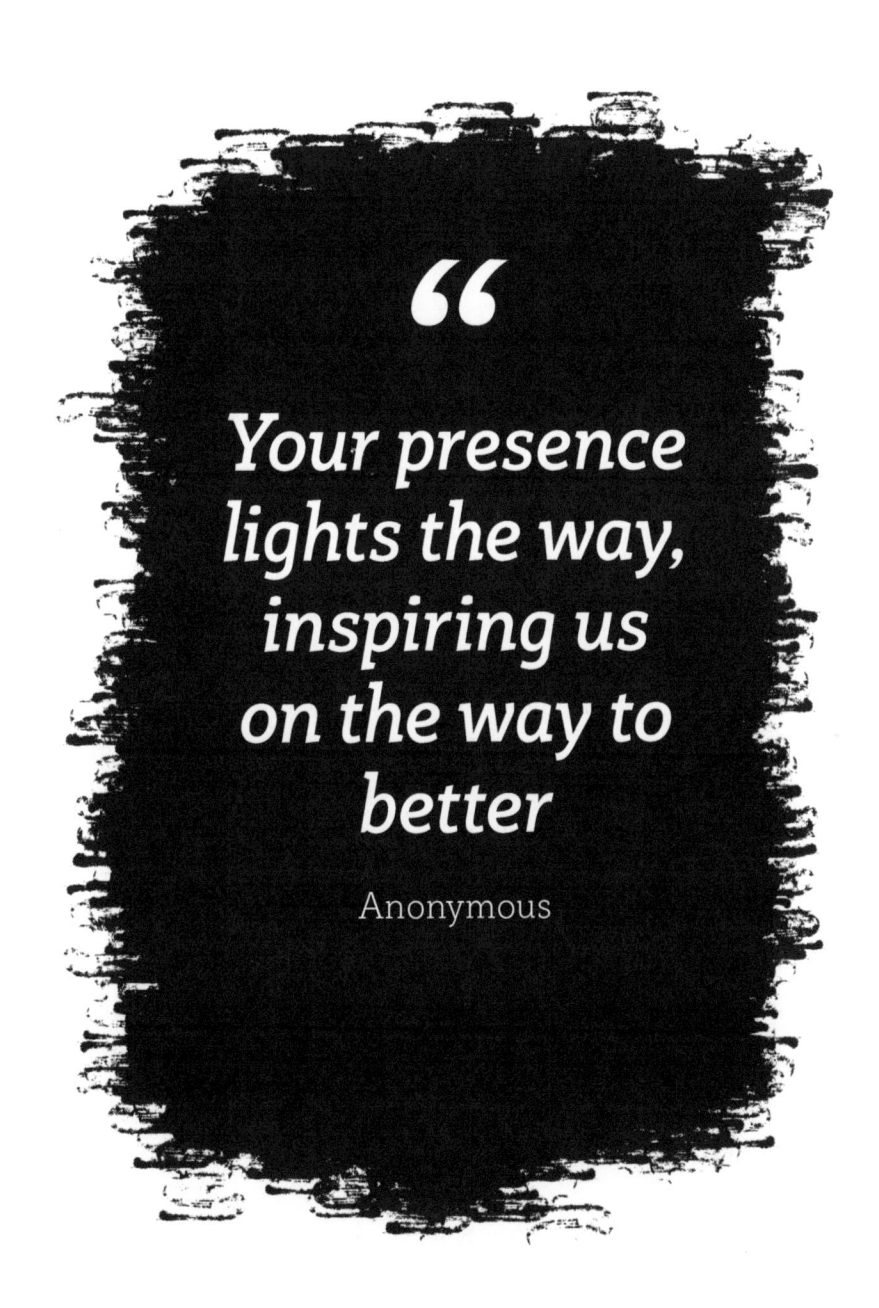

Anonymous

PICKING AND CHOOSING

Anonymous

Dear White Woman,

I'm not sure how to start this or what to say to you after years of feeling this way. But I am going to try.

The summer of 2020 was one of the darkest of my life. Not only was there a global pandemic claiming the lives of people around the world, but there was also a war waged against innocent Black bodies. Every day, I'd turn on the news and first see the death toll for COVID-19 and then, like clockwork, a video of a beautiful Black body being killed at the hands of someone who deemed them too dangerous, too threatening, too disposable.

It was exhausting. I'd go to work and have to deal with mundane tasks when there was a race war taking place outside my door. The week after the first protests, I had people asking me, "How was your weekend?" as if I hadn't spent it crying and cursing, trying to figure out why my skin was seen as less valuable than that of my white counterparts.

I also lost friends, many of whom look like you.

One, in particular, I'd been friends with for years, having played

PICKING AND CHOOSING

collegiate basketball with her. When I moved to Chicago, she was my go-to, my best friend, the person who showed me around the city and helped to get me settled.

We no longer speak.

When I needed her most, she was nowhere to be found. I had loose acquaintances texting and calling me, wanting to check in, yet she was silent, and her silence spoke volumes.

She comes from a wealthy Midwestern family and always claimed to be "fiscally conservative, but socially liberal" (first red flag). She has friends who are open Trump supporters, sporting their MAGA hats and drinking beers in front of their Trump flags, but still, I figured she was different.

I overlooked all of this because of the way most of her friends are people of color, or the way she only dates Black men, or the way she consumes Black music and culture. I assumed that when push came to shove, she'd show up for us because she took so much from us.

I was wrong.

In reality, amid the events of the summer, she chose to put her Whiteness first. She chose to sit back in her privilege and not engage, support, or show up. And when I chose to confront her about her silence, she became defensive, going with the typical, "You, a Black woman, are one of my best friends – how can I be racist?"

I share this story, not because I want you to feel bad for me, but because many of you are just like her. You pick and choose when you want to take part in Black culture (whether it be who you date or the aesthetic you appropriate), without truly caring about the people or communities that culture came from. When sh*t hits the fan, you choose to retreat into your comfort zone, leaving the very people you called friends left stranded and disheartened.

So, what can you do? In my eyes, you have two choices.

Choice #1: Become an unrelenting ally – do the work, educate yourself, listen to the experiences and stories of people who don't look like you, commit to being anti-racist in every facet of your life (and not just when it's convenient), and show up for your Black friends, colleagues, and acquaintances.

Choice #2: Become outwardly racist – wear your MAGA and alt-right gear, spew hatred and bigotry, don't associate with people of color, and wear your race on your sleeve – putting it before anyone or anything.

I know this may sound weird coming from a Black woman, but let me explain.

I give you these choices in order to protect myself. I'd rather know exactly what I'm getting into instead of being disappointed when you ultimately choose to sit in your privilege when this happens again.

At least this way I know, you were never on my side to begin with.

—The Friend You Left Behind

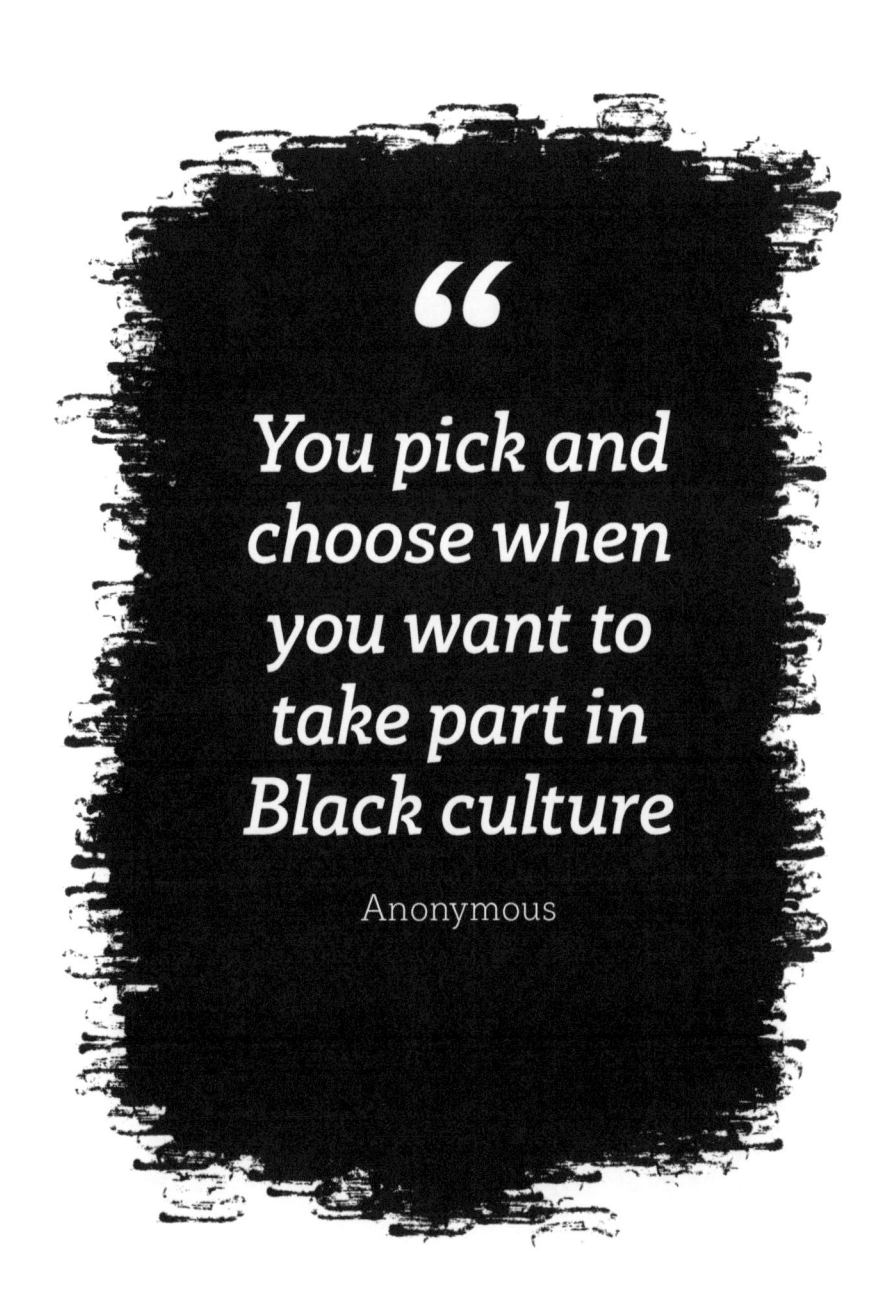

> **You pick and choose when you want to take part in Black culture**
>
> Anonymous

FORGING A KEY

Anonymous

Dear Black Woman,

Right now it's trendy for me to say I'm sorry. And I am. I am racist. And I am sorry. I am sorry for all of the infinite visible and invisible ways that I do harm to you because I don't fully see or don't fully understand – or even when I do understand, and I do it anyway because it's easier.

What's not so trendy is to say the other thing on my heart right now, that I believe is also true: that neither of us, neither you nor me, staying in committed relationships with our victimhood will not help us to stand in our power – the different kinds of power that each of us have – and take the next step to turn things around in our country and on our planet today.

It is the ultimate paradox. And I deeply want to be in this paradox with you. To mourn and heal the ways that we have been wounded. To stand up against and insist on the ending of the actions of the actors who have wounded us. And also to let go of our attachment to being right, when required, to ultimately reclaim the innate power that we also have always had, and always will.

I want to be held accountable to this level of truth and complexity.

FORGING A KEY

I want you to be fierce with me, when it's your truth and your desire to do so. I want you to expect that I know what microaggressions are. And at the moment when I perform one, if you feel compelled to tell me about it, I welcome your feedback, direct and raw. That f*cking hurt, and here's why.

But I also want you to know that I am committed to playing for both of our freedoms, even if it looks messy. Rather than saying exactly the right things that make me a good ally optically all the time (while secretly thinking I'm awesome for figuring out how to perform this White ally role so brilliantly fast), I want to acknowledge the complexity of intersectionality and explore all sides of the conversation, even at the risk of meeting your indignance or rage.

I want to risk doing it wrong. To throw out the handbook when it's time to really listen. To make mistakes, and even to challenge you sometimes, and to have that be the reason why we get closer. Why we get closer to being truly free.

I know that feeling your rage can be dangerous. That it may get you killed. May get you fired. May be the reason you're no longer able to pay the bills or feed your children. But I also know that physiologically, the path to healing trauma in the human body is to risk feeling your rage, taking action, and slowly discovering what's possible on the other side.

I want to be in this complex conversation with you. To untangle the prison that you and I both inhabit in different ways, when it comes to what we are not allowed to do, but is actually the pathway to our freedom and our healing.

I want you to feel my deep deep care when I show up for you

DEAR WHITE WOMAN, DEAR BLACK WOMAN

in those moments. In those moments, I want to be forgiven for the color of my skin, which I also didn't choose, and also held accountable in any ways necessary, for the privilege my Whiteness has afforded me.

And I want to be known for the prison that still binds me, as a good daughter of the patriarchy. That in all the ways it looks great from the outside, it's still a prison, and I am still in my own process of getting free.

I want you to know that despite all of my privilege, I may not be able to hand you certain keys that I don't possess. But I believe that, between the two of us, we may be able to *forge a key* from the broken metal parts that we each have tucked away in our pockets and forgot about for a very long time.

Dear Black Woman. I want you to know that I think you are important. You are beautiful. You're powerful. And you're needed. And I want you to know that I have your back.

Sincerely,
Anonymous White Woman

> *forge a key from the broken metal parts that we each have tucked away*
>
> Anonymous

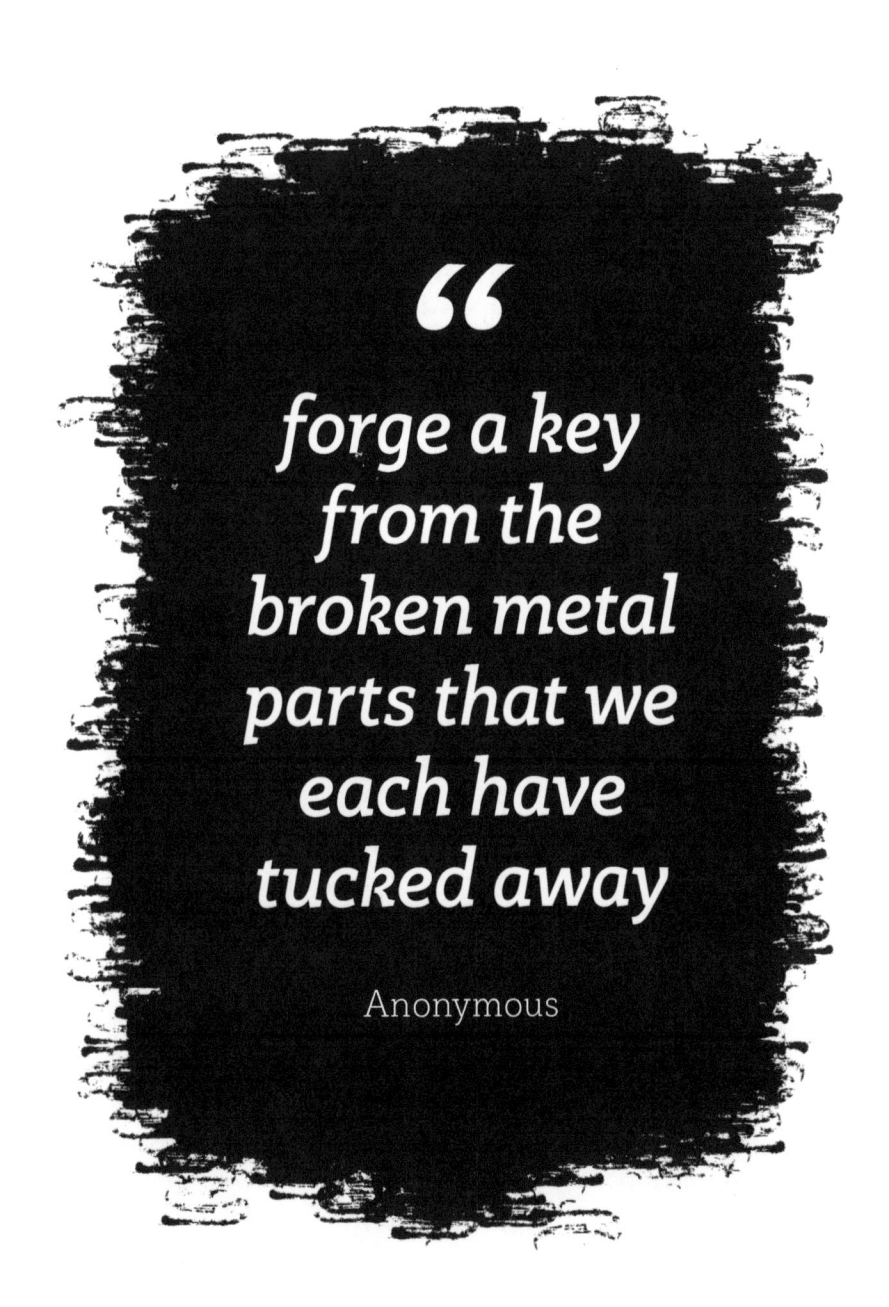

LIVING IN UNSPOKEN SEGREGATION

T. M.

Dear White Woman,

I was born in Harlem, and raised in the Bronx. I had the privilege to attend a private nursery school and Catholic elementary school through my first year of High School. The schools I had attended were predominantly African American and Latino. I didn't have much exposure to White people until I attended college and began working in Manhattan at the age of eighteen. New York City is considered a melting pot and therefore I didn't realize the majority of my life I lived in unspoken segregation. My neighborhoods were segregated by race and income level.

I didn't know what racism was until I had my first experience at ten years old. My family was on vacation in Elizabeth City, North Carolina, visiting a family member. This family member owned a large amount of land in this city and held great prestige in the community. One Saturday afternoon, she dropped my family off at a country club, in which she was a member. She had an appointment elsewhere and thought it would be a good idea to enjoy the amenities of the country club until her return. Unfortunately, we were not able to swim in the pool and therefore it was suggested we swim in the lake. I can't recall most of this visit to the country club, but I do remember feeling uncomfortable because we were the only Black people at the club. We were treated with subpar service and as outcasts due to the color of our skin. I witnessed a group of White teenage boys taunting my fourteen-year-old god sister. They asked her where she got her complexion from. At that moment, I felt a gut punch for her and myself at the realization that our skin color was a problem. My first experience with racism in Elizabeth City created a negative impression of White people. It changed my innocence as a child to fear White people because they believed they were better than Black people.

During my early twenties, I experienced racism living at my mother's home. It was located across from a police precinct in a historic part of the Bronx, where the majority of the detectives were White males who did not live in my neighborhood. They would disrespect the homeowners by parking in their driveways and double parked to the point where trash pickup became a problem. The detectives were assigned a parking lot nearby but refused to park there.

One late night, I came home with friends. There was a detective's vehicle parked in my mom's driveway in front of the gate. I went into the precinct to ask for the vehicle to be moved. Sadly, this was a common practice on my block. Once the car was moved, I pulled my vehicle into the driveway. After getting out of the car, I heard a detective standing in front of the precinct and yelled out, "You made him move so you can park there?" Followed by another detective yelling "yeah" out of the window. Immediately, I was enraged by their privileged behavior and began to yell back at the detectives. I yelled out that I lived at this home and could park there if I wanted to. One of them yelled that their fellow detective should not have moved their vehicle to allow me to park. I yelled back stating, I lived at this property, and they did not. Also, I continued to yell, "I bet that your neighborhood doesn't look like this block" and how they disrespect the homeowners by parking anywhere they want in my neighborhood. The detectives threatened that they would raid my home. The next day, I told my mom about this encounter and she filed a complaint with the precinct's sergeant. Ironically, during this time, I lived less than ten minutes away from a young African man, Amadou Diallo[1], who lost his life at the hands of police officers. He was shot and killed in front of his home due to mistaken identity.

Dear White Woman... I have shared a couple of life-altering experiences that have caused some form of trauma, all due to my race. I would ask you to understand a Black woman has to battle sexism, racism, misogyny, and discrimination in our everyday lives. We encounter stress by being the backbone of the Black family. We experience stress at work by being disregarded in the workplace starting with pay. Historically, Black women receive the least amount of pay even if they are overqualified for the position.[2] Black women also witness White women excel in the workplace due to White privilege. White women privilege will also lead some to feel above Black women even though they have the same title. White women's privilege is a superpower and is typically used for the wrong purpose.

White woman, I ask that you reflect on your childhood about race. Did you have to witness or endure a situation referring to the color of your skin? Did you live oblivious to race until adulthood? Do you have empathy for minority communities including the Black community? My call to action is that you educate yourself on the Black/African American experience. Be empathetic to a Black woman. Choose to understand a Black woman may go through more trials in her lifetime than you would ever witness. If ever you have the opportunity, use your White woman privilege to help a Black woman... lift her up.

Thank you for taking the time to read my letter. I hope it has brought some clarity and understanding about a Black Woman.

Sincerely,
T. M.
Atlanta, Georgia

---

[1] 2022. "Amadou Diallo Killed by Police." HISTORY. January 24, 2022. https://www.history.com/this-day-in-history/amadou-diallo-killed-by-police-new-york-city.

[2] Review of Highlights of Women's Earnings in 2023. 2024. BLS Reports: U.S. Bureau of Labor and Statistics. https://www.bls.gov/opub/reports/womens-earnings/2023/.

> *I lived in unspoken segregation*
>
> T.M.

FINDING MY PLACE IN THE SOLUTION

Rachel

Dear Black Woman,

I remember when we first met. I saw you dancing on the sidewalk outside our dormitory with your friends. You all were lined up in a row dancing, singing, and chanting. We were freshmen in college, it was move-in day. Something connected y'all together and I could feel it. I was not sure what that dance meant to you, but it didn't matter. I could tell you were sisters, connected in many ways that I would not understand.

You were beautiful, dear Black Woman. Your hair was big and your smile was confident. You were laughing, all of you were laughing and singing and being so loud. I loved it! You had just met each other and yet you were friends. I was jealous in that moment of your community, your connection that I didn't understand.

Dear Black Woman your power is tremendous, you are a powerful, strong, and capable force. Today, I work with you. I watch you do more than anyone else with the same skills and job. Your voice seems quieter than it was on that day outside my college dormitory. One moment, I struggle to understand why, and ask myself *where are you? Where has that force gone that*

DEAR WHITE WOMAN, DEAR BLACK WOMAN

I saw on move-in day in Oklahoma? Another moment I see the oppression you fight every single day, all day. I bet you are tired; I know you are tired.

I see you and I acknowledge your struggle and struggle to find my place in the solution. I fear for your children and acknowledge my children's role in your oppression. It hurts and I am angry as hell about it. Yet, I struggle to find my place in the solution. I want to hug you; I stand in the street and fight for you. I talk to my senators and, yet, nothing happens. Yet again, I struggle to find my place in the solution.

Dear Black Woman, as we share more similarities than differences please do not give up. I do not plan to give up. Though I am constantly struggling to see myself in the solution, I promise you I will not contribute to the problem. I will tell my kids your stories, I will tell them about meeting you that day in college. I will tell them about your oppression and teach them better than I was taught. I will tell them about your power. I will not stop until I see a solution. Until we are equal in our struggles, I will not stop.

In Grace,
Rachel
Pea Ridge, Arkansas

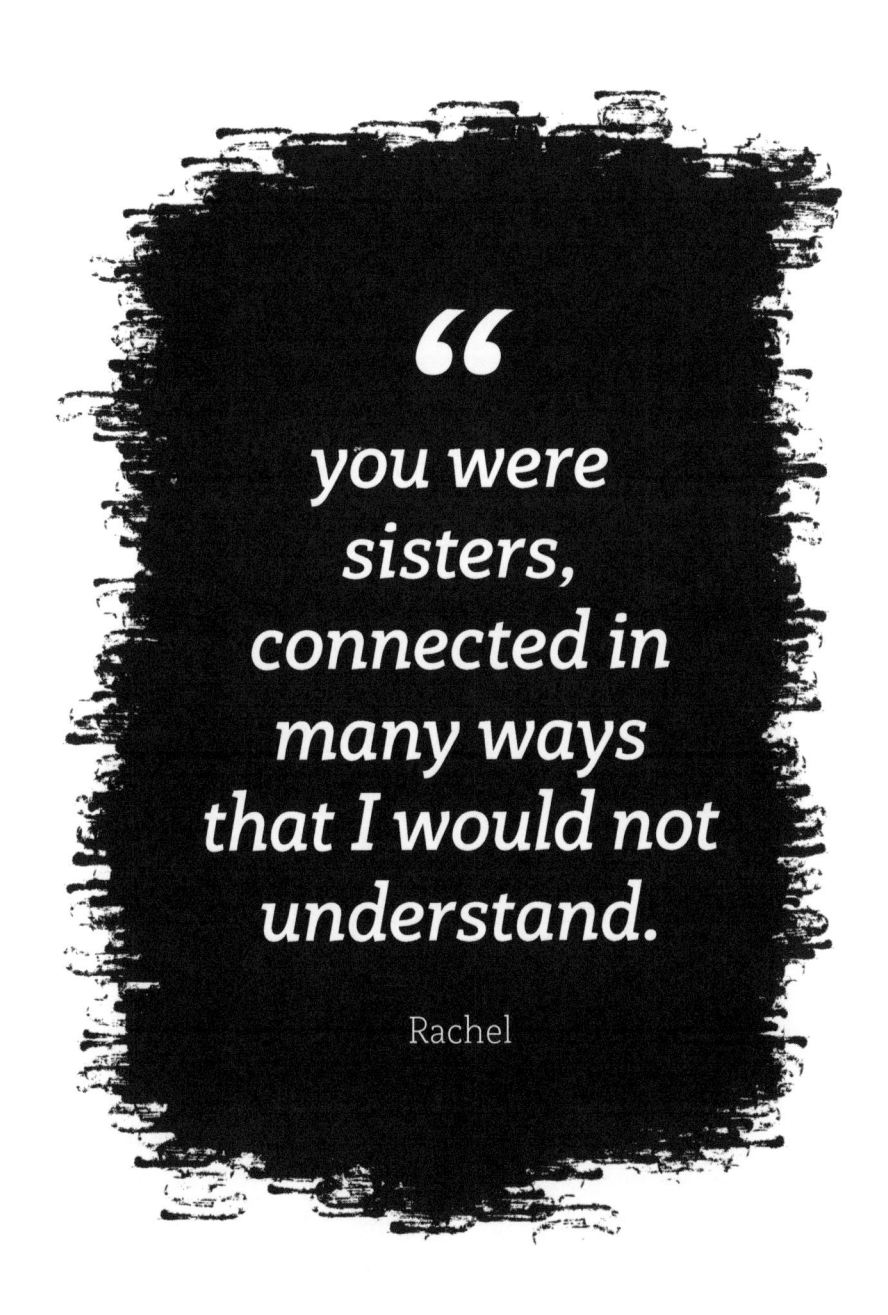

> **you were sisters, connected in many ways that I would not understand.**
>
> Rachel

NO MATTER WHAT

Anonymous

Dear White Woman,

As I sit and reflect on this tumultuous year, it goes to show that your privilege is beyond my wildest dreams. As a mother, educator, wife, and mentor, it sickens me to see that you're valued more than the little Brown and Black babies who call me teacher, call me mom, and call me auntie.

The election of the 45th President was enough to show that your privilege is all that matters to you. You got out there and voted in such large amounts, and sadly you were proud. You know the Amerikkkan way.

See, the issue here is that you believe that you are more valuable than me and the women who stand up to injustices day in and day out. We have paved the way and are always the saving grace. As we stand on the forefront for our Black males and fight injustices, you are home, safe, and sound. Tucked away in your bed as we are pepper sprayed, shot, and killed. Your child does not have to fear walking to the store for Skittles, playing loud music, selling loose cigarettes, sleeping in their bed after a long day of work, being "awkward," dancing, jogging, having a mental illness, and my God, the list goes on and on. The amount of lives lost just for the common daily activity is sickening, but yet again,

NO MATTER WHAT

it proudly displays your privilege. You know, like the flags you proudly display in your front yards.

You're seen as superior to me. No matter the time or day I will always be considered less than you. I will always be considered not worthy. Your child will always be superior to my child. Her curls will be the reason she is teased. Her melanin-filled skin will be the reason she is teased. Day in and day out, I recite affirmations with a one-year-old. Why? Because I want her to know that no matter what, she is important, she is worthy, and she is somebody.

I hope that by reading this letter you understand that the privilege you have surpasses my worth to society. Take time to realize that you can be an agent of change. While you come to this realization be sure to include your children in this shift because they will be next up. Your privilege will always stick with you as long as you're White, so at least use it for good.

I ask that you take the time to raise your children with decency. I ask that you teach them not to use their privilege for evil. I ask that you teach them not to be a bystander when out in the world. I ask that you teach them to fight for justice, to fight for equality, to fight for equity, and to fight for liberation.

Signed,
A Tired Black Woman
Hyattsville, Maryland

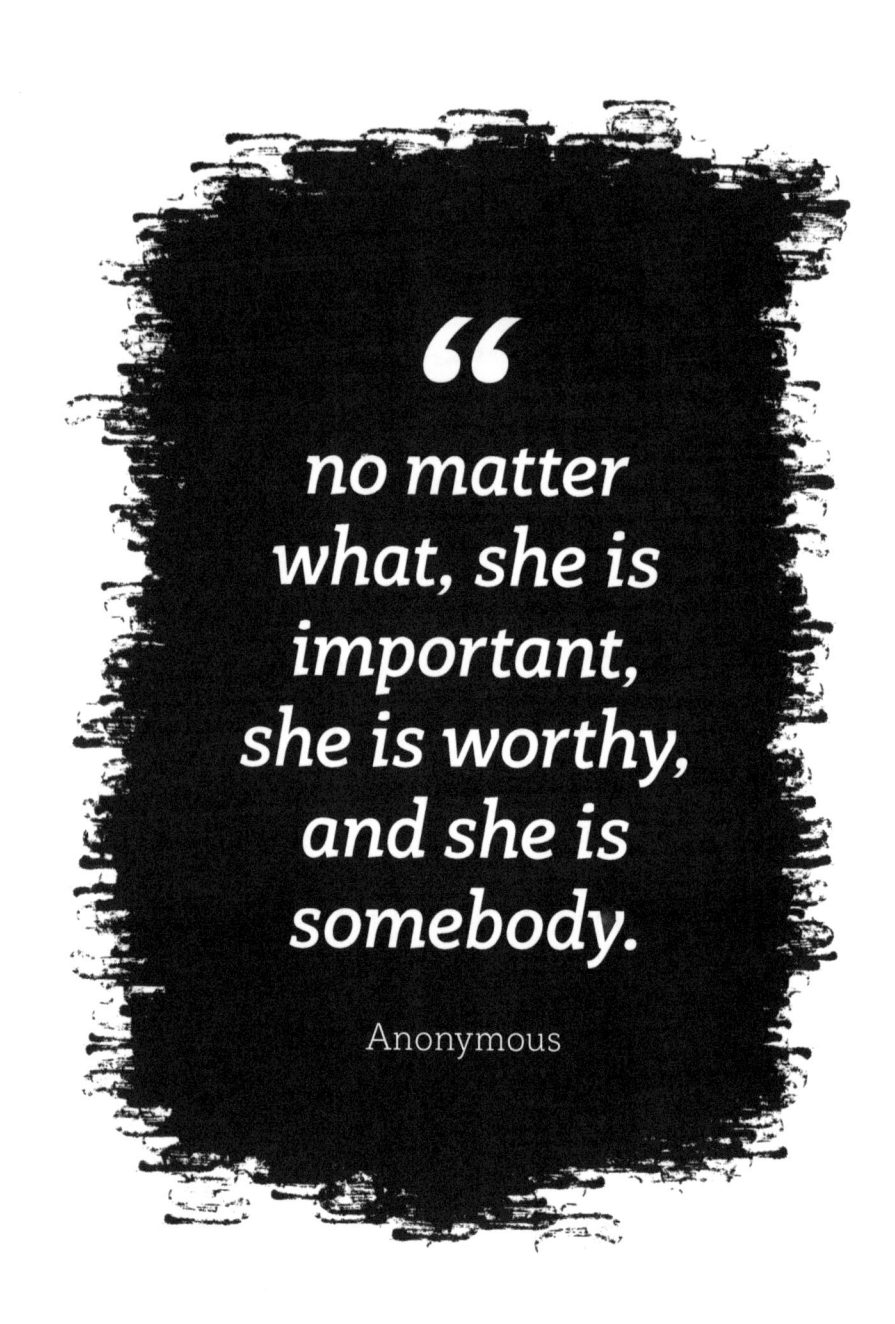

> *no matter what, she is important, she is worthy, and she is somebody.*

Anonymous

WHEN ACTION CAUSES MORE HARM THAN GOOD

Barbara

Dear Black Woman,

I write this letter with a mix of trepidation and excitement to those of you whom I know and those I will never meet. I am deeply honored to have been asked to share. As I reflect on the journey that has brought me here, I feel a profound sense of responsibility in my words and gratitude for the experiences I have had.

First and foremost, I owe you a sincere apology for past actions and inactions that have diminished and marginalized Black women. I am aware that I cannot undo the hurt that has been caused, but I want to acknowledge it and express my heartfelt regret for not doing better.

I am also deeply grateful for the grace you have offered me, and for the lessons which I have learned through working with and for Black women over the years. Your authentic joy, forgiveness, love, and steadfast commitment to justice have profoundly impacted me. I have made many mistakes along the way–mistakes I cannot even fully remember. Thanks to your patience and guidance, I have learned and grown from them.

While I cannot speak for all White women, I can share that I have perpetuated and witnessed harm that has been inflicted and, at times, failed to interrupt it. This letter is my attempt to confront that reality and to acknowledge my own fear in doing so. I realize that my fear is small compared to the challenges and traumas you and your ancestors have endured.

I believe in the impact of intergenerational trauma and the urgent need to end racism. I understand that my role is to set aside my fear of discomfort, to lean in, and to actively resist and work to reverse the dominance of white culture. I am committed to stepping back and allowing Black women to lead, to building authentic relationships, and to not speaking over you.

I pledge to be an ally who listens, learns, and supports. My goal is to continually strive to be better, not only in my actions but in my heart. I am committed to working towards a more equitable and just society and to ensuring that my efforts are meaningful and impactful toward ending White supremacist culture.

Thank you for the opportunity to learn from you and to grow alongside you. I am dedicated to making this journey one of genuine support and progress.

With deep respect and gratitude,
Barbara
Hamburg Township, Michigan

WHEN ACTION CAUSES MORE HARM THAN GOOD

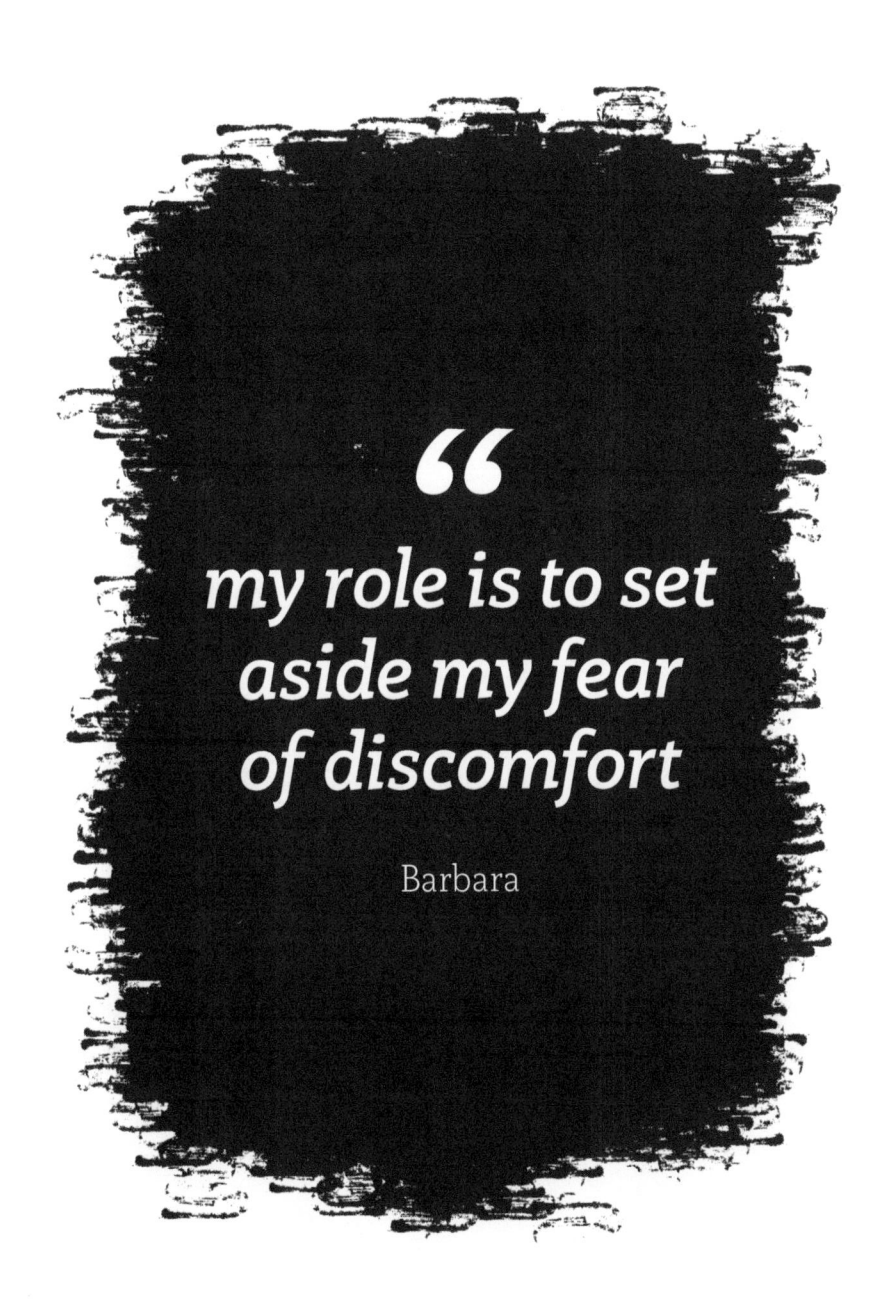

> *my role is to set aside my fear of discomfort*
>
> Barbara

SEEING ME IN THIS FIGHT

Anonymous

Dear White Woman,

I'm writing this letter to the many White women in my family and the White women who are my friends– in hopes that you will further see me, my truth, and use my words to continue advocating for me and other Black women as strong, "woke" allies.

I also write this to the White women who educated me, attended school with me, women I work (and worked) with, attended church small groups with, and randomly encountered throughout daily life. It is many of these White women who showed me what racism, disrespect, privilege, and discrimination look like and feel like. I am writing this to you in hopes that you will see that your interactions with me, were indeed, racist–as you attempted to exert power and dominance over me. In these moments, you're also showing me, that in the progressive women's movement that you're so dedicated to, you don't see me in this fight. Because if you did, you would see me and respect me as a woman, as a sister.

To both types of White women in my life, my intention here is to share who I am and how I must navigate this world. As I prepared to write this, I thought back to elementary school–where I was the only Black person in my class, and I first realized my race was the reason for how I was being treated. The other girls in class didn't talk to me, didn't play with me, and felt as if I was invisible. I remember asking myself, do *they see me?*

Over the years, in high school, graduate school, and entering the workforce, and even right now as a corporate executive, my exchanges with most White women have me asking myself, *Do they see me?* Do they see me when I flashed a friendly smile and it was disregarded? Do they see the title on my door and in my signature line, when they (several levels below me in the org structure) tell me why what I'm doing is wrong, berate me in an email, or suggest I do not know what I am doing? Do they hear me when I am talking and still choose to talk over me? Do they realize that the "prove me wrong" mentality is offensive because it assumes that they're "subtly" waiting for me to fail?

Do you see that in those situations–which happen multiple times in a **day**–that my contributions are considered inconsequential, and there is an overt attempt to render my expertise irrelevant? It makes me feel that the reason these women can't champion me or root for me is because they think they should be excelling before me–after all, what they know and see is that they're White and that I'm Black. Of course, I don't know if this is the definitive reason. All I can speak to is my experience and observations of how those White women treat others versus how I've been treated.

So now, I'll ask you. . .do you want to see me? And if you do, what are you ready to see me as? A woman just like you? Black – different from you? Or, are you ready to see me for me–a Black woman who is equal to you?

When you do see me–truly see me–you will see that our struggles to achieve equality, and equity as women are drastically different. When you walk into a room, people likely notice your gender or age first. When I walk into a room, my Blackness is noted first, even by you. And because of this, the solidarity and unity that we are supposed to have as women, fades away.

Now, don't get me wrong. I do want you to see my Blackness. I don't want you to be color-blind.

But as Mellody Hobson says, I want you to be color brave. You are seeing a woman whose natural hair, body shape and skin tone have been ridiculed for centuries only to now be trendy and emulated. You are seeing a woman who, on the exterior, must be incredibly strong for everyone. but on the inside, is tired. I'm tired of having to take the high road when you are disrespectful or do not collaborate with me despite my countless attempts. I'm tired of having to put my best foot forward though maintaining the status quo for others is permissible. I am proud of who I am and why I am, but I am tired of having to prove my worth.

When you do see me–truly see me–you will see, that I am not your competition. I am not a threat to your existence. My self-advocacy, big-picture thinking, and holding you (and others) accountable is not at attack on you– it's how I deliver the results I've been entrusted and the excellence that's been engrained in me to exude.

Why is it that we as women share a commonality but are often worlds apart? We must fix this. I'm in. Are you?

Here's what I commit to: ensuring I continue giving people the benefit of the doubt until proven otherwise. I know (and act in accordance with this) that not all White women are *those kinds of White women*. And though I am tired, I will continue to take the high road. I will not be silent. I will not be the professor and educate them about every aspect of my being, but, I will show them how this Black woman, committed to empowering all women, conducts herself and honors herself while uplifting others.

I am committed to showing you who I am. You will see all that I am driven, passionate, amazing, smart, funny, nonjudgmental, and an amazingly loyal friend. You will see that I do not look at my history solely as one of hurt and sorrow, but of ingenuity and perseverance. You will see that when we join forces, we can be incredibly powerful. I will show you, me.

I hope you are ready to truly see me and respect me.

Sincerely,
A Woman to be Seen

> **"are you ready to see me for me**

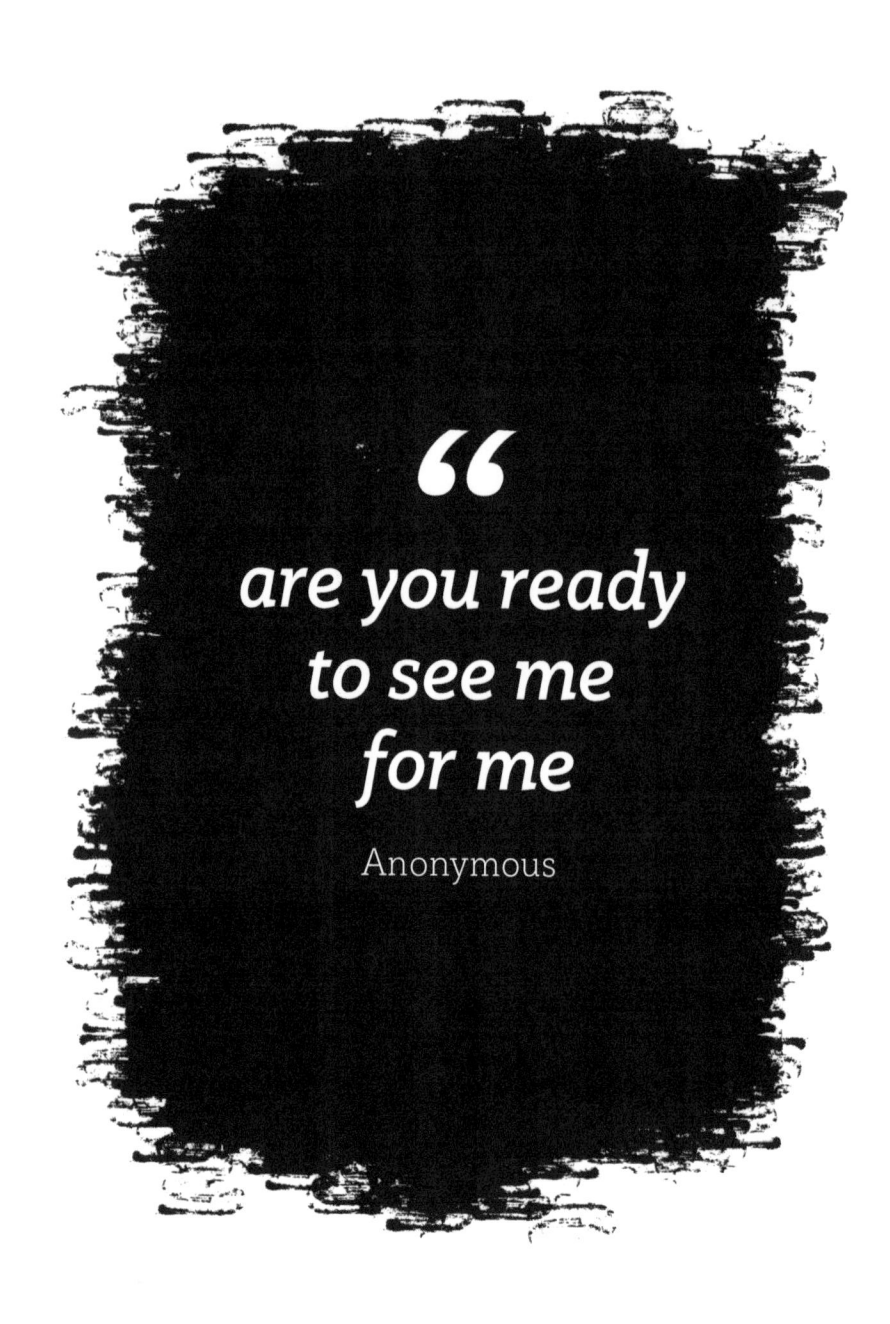

— Anonymous

THE MULTICOLOR COMMUNAL TABLE

Sabine

Dear Black Woman... no, Dear Black Sister,

Being a sister can be the best thing on the planet – unconditional love, happiness, bottomless silliness, meaningful fun, inspiration to reach for the stars, undoubted support, a partner-in-crime who always has your back, yet never asks for favors in return. We make each other feel whole. We belong together.

Being a sister is also hard – sometimes we fight because we ignore boundaries, expect too much, take without asking, don't appreciate each other's big and little gestures, and compete for attention and affection. We take it for granted. And sometimes we are made to second-guess, question, or even envy.

Why? Who does that serve? Why do we allow that?

I grew up in Germany, the oldest of three sisters, in a neighborhood run by "typical boys" (and me), went to an all-girls school surrounded by strong, independent, role-model women (and extraordinary male teachers) who raised me to follow in their footsteps, think, speak up, serve my neighbors, and leave the world a better place than I found it.

Everything I knew about ethnicity and race in the U.S. came from watching Sesame Street on German TV and my history and ethics courses. I watched diverse communities care for and take care of one another on Sesame Street. I was taught about expressions of caring behavior that carries across religions and about communities where people of every ethnic origin and creed live side by side in "the melting pot." And I learned about the Civil Rights Movement, Martin Luther King Jr., his philosophy of nonviolent change making and his vision of the Beloved Community. I thought Atlanta had figured it out. Until I moved to the U.S. when I was twenty and my one-year exchange turned into a permanent arrangement. I had to build a new life, a new community around me with sisters and brothers, coaches, inspiring role-models, etc. A bit naive, I thought that was an easy thing to do in this melting pot . . . until I began taking a closer look.

I am White but not a typical suburban White who votes against public transit initiatives because they are afraid of "the people in the city" coming out to destroy their pristine neighborhoods. I didn't fit in. I am a Christian, but not the type that condemns others for their choices. I didn't fit in. I volunteered at my kids' schools and local nonprofits and didn't fit in. I am a caucasian American . . . and I am German . . . and I am a world citizen because of my lived experiences. My frame of reference is different, it's mine.

Race, our skin color, is such an arbitrary, shallow, bizarre line to draw. It's even more arbitrary, shallow, and bizarre to maintain it in this day and age! I open my mouth, my mind, and my heart and find more commonalities with my sisters from Colombia, Kenya, Ghana, the Caribbean Islands, France, Korea regardless of skin tone or religion or mother tongue. I have learned to communicate with my Canadian, Indian, and Hispanic neighbors and know that I adjust my communication style to find commonalities. The world is interesting and beautiful because of all the shades and nuances we bring to the communal table.

And I know all of us want the same thing: safe neighborhoods where we can raise our children like cousins, where they can take advantage of any and all opportunities this country has to offer – education, medical care, professions, careers, etc.

But . . . it's one thing to know what's right and a whole different thing to do the right thing. It's easy to do nothing and incredibly hard to do something – especially if that's against the normal order of things. I didn't build what we are dealing with. After thirty years, I still don't fully understand all the ramifications, and I don't like what I see.

As an immigrant I will probably never understand why people adhere to traditions that don't serve them, why the system still is what it is. How do we bring to light, discuss, and work on a system that is built on the premise of differences, class, order, hierarchy, and exploitation and that persists on division, intentional lack of access, and mistrust and isn't going to make it possible to create value for all, for us to be sisters . . . easily . . . without change . . . without determined work? I don't know how to change it by myself but I am here to be a part of the change and support those with solutions.

"All for one, one for all" is the motto attributed to legendary musketeers, but I know that we women operate on this principle. You are my tribe, my family. Period. Don't mess with one of mine or else.

I never liked my very light skin. I glow in the moonlight to a degree that attracts moths and bugs that fly into my face and hair, and I can't stand it. For as long as I can remember I wanted to have darker skin and anything but my spaghetti curls. My friends and I roasted on tanning beds and used toxic chemicals to perm our hair. Once I had daughters I began to wonder, *why do we dislike or even hate our own features?* How does it start, and how is it reinforced? Media, yes of course, but how do we talk to each other? Have you received or given the advice to wear something else to hide your less than perfect XYZ? Instead, can we shift our advice to focus on developing and accentuating our best features? "You have beautiful eyes, when they shine nothing else matters. How can I help you shine when you walk out the door, have to present, ace the interview, etc.?"

With two sisters at home, BFFs, and hundreds of classmates of all ages, sizes, backgrounds and interests, I am aware of sisterly tensions but I learned early on that we can overcome anything and accomplish everything we set our minds to. What we need is commitment to an environment and resources where that is possible.

I want to be your sister in the fullest sense. I want to ensure that each of us are able to learn about ourselves and find our best selves, that we take time to celebrate each other, and that we have the opportunity to create communities where we, our daughters and nieces, sons and nephews, our grandchildren belong.

A long time ago a coach told me: you are always welcome to tell me about your challenge, your frustration, but always come equipped with at least three possible ways to address the challenge together. Consciously or unconsciously, this coach instilled in me that I have influence over the outcome. It established the locus of control in me. Girls and women don't automatically take the backseat. Girls and women don't wait for help. Girls and women are more often in charge than we give ourselves credit for. We create and grow the communities we live in. Let's do it!

What is it that you see and understand?
Which talent and interest do you have that provides an answer to our challenge?
What do you have influence on?
What do you have control over?
What do you need assistance with?

It's always good to be heard but it's empowering to know that I have the ability to kick off incremental change. I hear you, and I am looking forward to a future where all of us hear each other and support each other to create flourishing communities, with safety, opportunity, education, and neighborly love, where each and every one of us can thrive to their fullest.

With Support,
Sabine

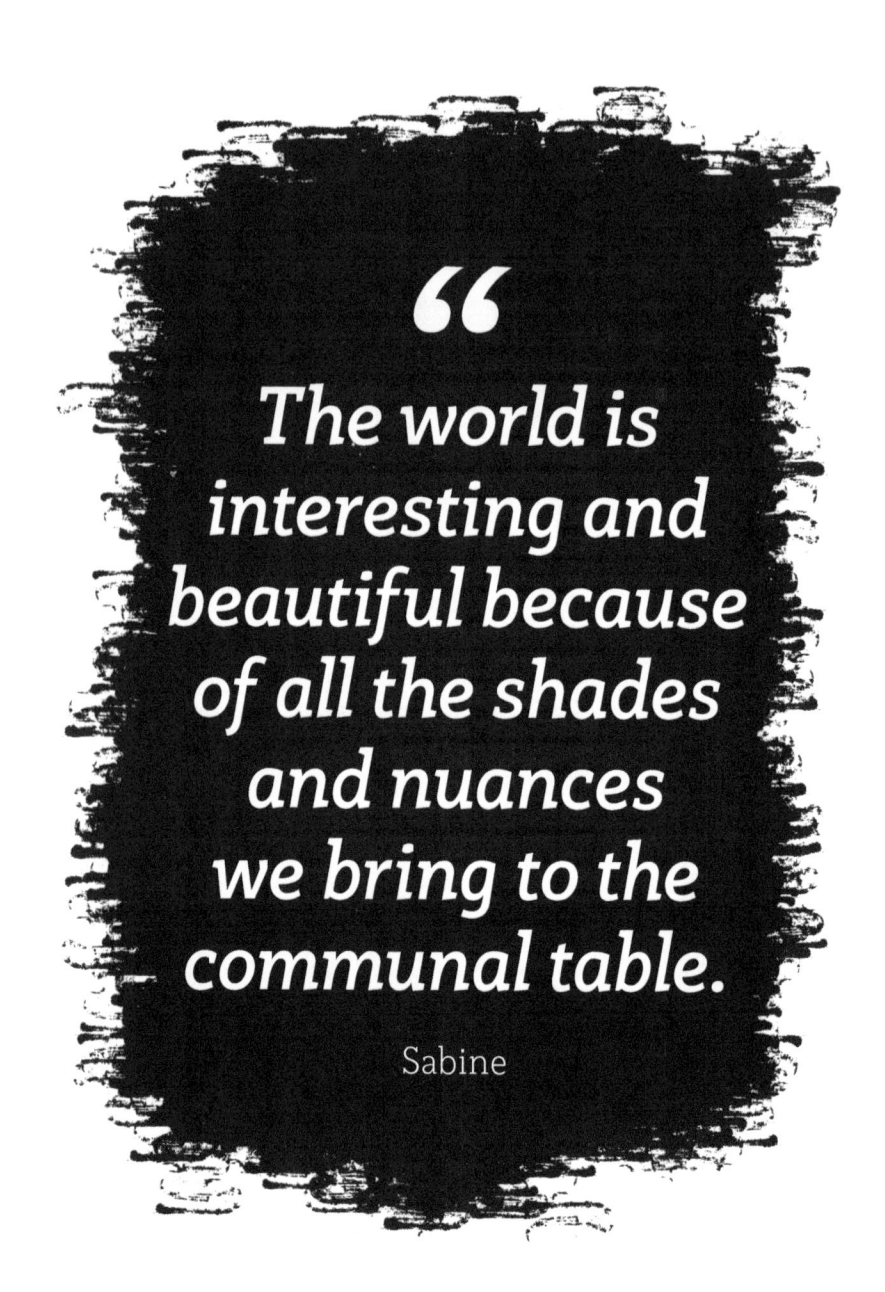

> "The world is interesting and beautiful because of all the shades and nuances we bring to the communal table.
>
> Sabine

AN ABUNDANCE OF ALLYSHIP

Althea

Dear White Woman,

I choose to write my letter from a place and space of **allyship.**

> To ensure that we are all on the same page, "allyship" is defined as: "the practice of emphasizing social justice, inclusion, and human rights by members of an **ingroup** (typically but not always, White women), to advance the interests of an oppressed or marginalized **outgroup** (typically, Black women or any women of color/non-White). Although there are plenty of examples where women within the same outgroup oppress or marginalize one another also, based on color and social status. Allyship is part of the anti-oppression movement or anti-racist conversation, which puts into use social justice theories and ideals." [1]

Why did I choose allyship? Because all women, regardless of race, ethnicity, nationality, religious beliefs, sexuality and gender preferences, socioeconomic status, or other factors, share similar experiences. We are born of women. Often, but not always, we are raised and nurtured by women. A matriarch typically leads the family (think, traditional family structures, down to the elephants and the orcas). Often, we learn how to "be women" from other women, whether that teaching is successful or unsuccessful. We navigate through the challenges of being women in similar ways, e.g., development from adolescence through puberty to adult womanhood, securing that first training bra, getting your menstrual cycle for the first time, the highs, and lows of our first relationships, for many having a first baby, etc. Many of the experiences for women are experiences most men **will never have.** These experiences should create a universal bond among all women, whether you meet your sister on the physical journey or not.

I believe we are allies in the larger struggle. Against what struggle might you ask? The struggle against male misogynistic attitudes about what it means to be a woman and therefore, what women should, and should not be allowed to do. Look at how Liz Cheney is being treated (aka "dragged") as a Caucasian woman, who was the leader of the GOP Republican Party Conference. She stepped out of line and the male misogynistic movement quickly put her back in place and stripped her of her power.

My White sister, why then would any of you oppress or support the oppression of any other woman again, regardless of her race, ethnicity, nationality, religious beliefs, sexuality, or socioeconomic status? Why would you support men and even other women, in the oppression of another woman? Why would you title her, belittle and shame her, limit her and reduce her existence and experiences to squalor and poverty and hunger, to use your vote and use governmental policies to stifle her voice, her access to healthcare and education, her access to fair and affordable housing, her ability to be hired and promoted and create wealth for herself and her family, her ability to be safe in her community and not subject to violence and the constant and systemic fear that comes with being a woman (being gobbled up

AN ABUNDANCE OF ALLYSHIP

by a man), and more crucial to a women of color?

I realize a lot of this behavior stems from your own fears that if I am not the oppressor, then I will next be the oppressed. If I do not align myself with the oppressor, then he (or she) will also turn and oppress me next. Instead, might we consider joining forces as the **collective** of women and overcome the overseer, the oppressor, and work to create community for all women where we can be happy, healthy and safe? Create policies that build one another up and take care of one another, so we can in turn care for ourselves and families.

I learned once in a session led by Dr. Barbara King (Leader, Hillside Faith Center, Atlanta, GA) this belief system – there is no lack or limitation; the universe has an abundance of everything that everyone needs.

In closing, women do not need to oppress one another to maintain our selves. We need to promote and adopt allyship and work for the betterment of all women.

Thank you,
Althea

---

[1] 2024. "Allyship." Wikipedia.

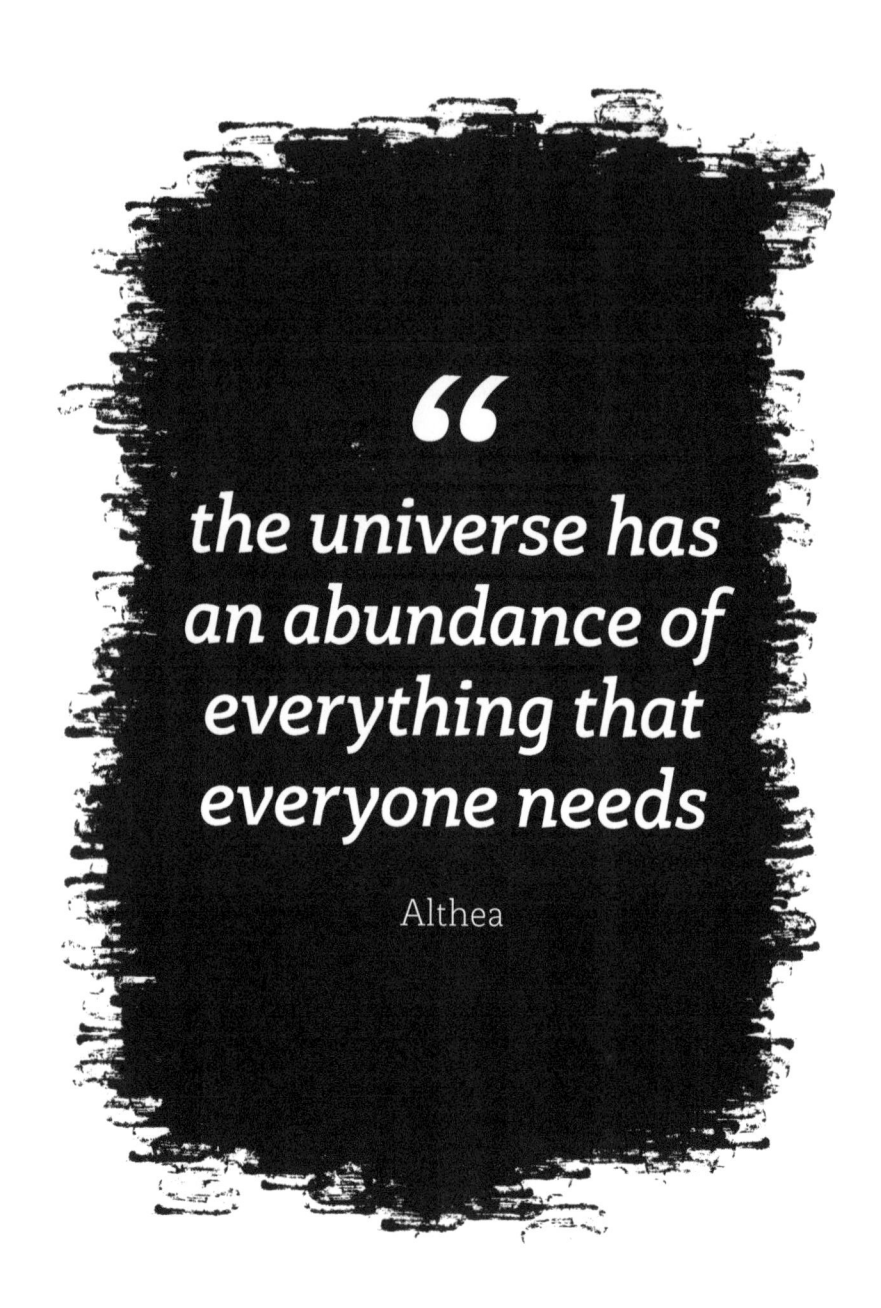

> **the universe has an abundance of everything that everyone needs**
>
> Althea

A STUDENT IN SEARCH OF TRUTH

Gail

Dear Black Woman,

"I guess the only time most people think about injustice, is when it happens to them." – *Charles Bukowski*

Since the graphic cellphone video of the brutal murder of George Floyd, I believe many more people worldwide felt it was happening to them.

It certainly awakened me; I began watching the related broadcasts and staring for hours at the protesters, especially those down the street from me, in Atlanta. There I saw a poster being carried with words I'd never seen before:

WHITE SILENCE IS VIOLENCE.

It resonated with me immediately, but so did the fear that I would say all the wrong things.

I did not trust myself to connect with my Black friends, but silence was no longer an option. Thank goodness for the Internet. I don't even remember what I "Googled" but help was on the way. I quickly found an article, written by a Black man headlined "White

Friends, Don't Send Us Heart Emojis." I read it and realized that I had a text ready to go containing exactly that. His warning went on to suggest, "Don't invite us to share-all; if we want to express our feelings to you, we'll let you know . . ."

Following this insight, I completely changed the narrative of my text. It was no longer about protecting my feelings, out of fear of offending. It was and is, about listening and being receptive.

While searching for additional direction, I joined 300 others in an online course entitled "Spiritual Allyship: Dismantling Racism through Bravery, Humility, and Bringing Forth the Voices of the Unheard" and conducted by Rev. Derica Blackmon.* I showed up each of the seven weeks and learned, among other things, about microaggressions. Some of these slights were previously lost on me.

I also watched the 1992 landmark Oprah Winfrey Show, featuring the diversity-educator Jane Elliott, best known for the "Blue Eyes, Brown Eyes Experiment." Shock ran through me as I got in touch with the ignorance, obliviousness, and hostility, held by many Whites, who were inflicting harm as a result; me included.

I then became a student aimed at understanding racial injustice, and began reading; *Black Like Me, White Fragility, Stamped from The Beginning,* and others. I also watched films, including *Woke, Freedom Summer,* and *Mississippi Justice.*

Please know that going forward, I will stay on this path of education in search of truth, understanding, and change.

Sincerely,
Gail

*Affiliated with The Shift Network

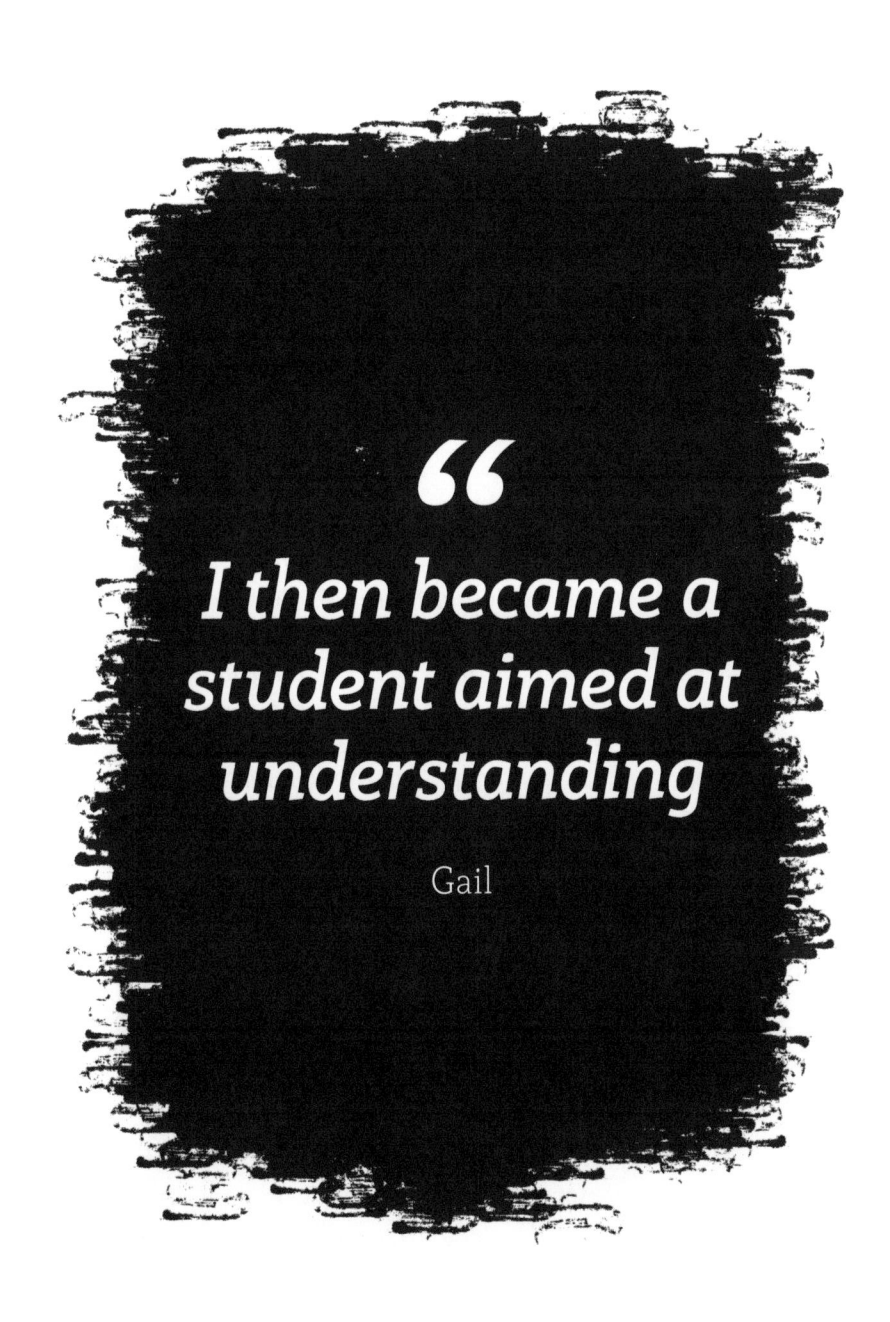

> "*I then became a student aimed at understanding*"
>
> Gail

IT'S TIME TO GET UNCOMFORTABLE

Attallah

Dear White Woman,

Imagine me writing this letter, with your feelings in mind thinking, *What would be palatable for White women? What would they like?* I'm not doing that NO MORE! Yes, I used double negatives! I have spent years of my life educating and nurturing your children, knowing full well you didn't see me as a complete human being. You only saw me as my service toward you. And that is the way you see people of color. The woman at the soul food truck, the colorful entertainers that bring you so much joy. But how do you show up when you're just walking your dog in your neighborhood?

Every single time you walk down the street please know there is some semblance of a place prepared for you. Sometimes I think, *Do we have any more in common, than the fact that we have vaginas or identify as women?* Is that enough?

My dearest White woman, the supposed epitome of womanhood, how do you advocate for others? Let's be frank, the reason racism is still a thing is in part because of your continued support/ partnership with White men in their upholding of systemic and institutional racism. Yes, your White men. You are married to them. They are your fathers, your pastors, brothers, sons, uncles, and grandfathers. You are protecting them just because they are close to you. Stop telling us about that "racist family member" that you still engage with. You ignore their abuses of power; you even applaud it. You laugh and mock Black people with your jokes and so-called sisterhood. And I'm not your "sis." You would treat a sister better than this.

Let's be real, we know you're oppressed too. I also ask you; how do you advocate for those who also identify as women?

You know what to do, gather **each other.** Hold each other accountable. In your homes, at the playdates, at your children's schools, at your places of worship, at your private clubs, and institutions.

You let that orange-ade monster slide through, the archetype of a White man.

Some of us happen to not be White, some of us happen to be queer POC. Black People. We are also indigenous people; you know, the ones who were here before you got here. Here. All over the world.

We didn't start this fire, but we are burning. We invented fires and will burn for evermore.

Present,
Attallah

> "You only saw me as my service toward you.

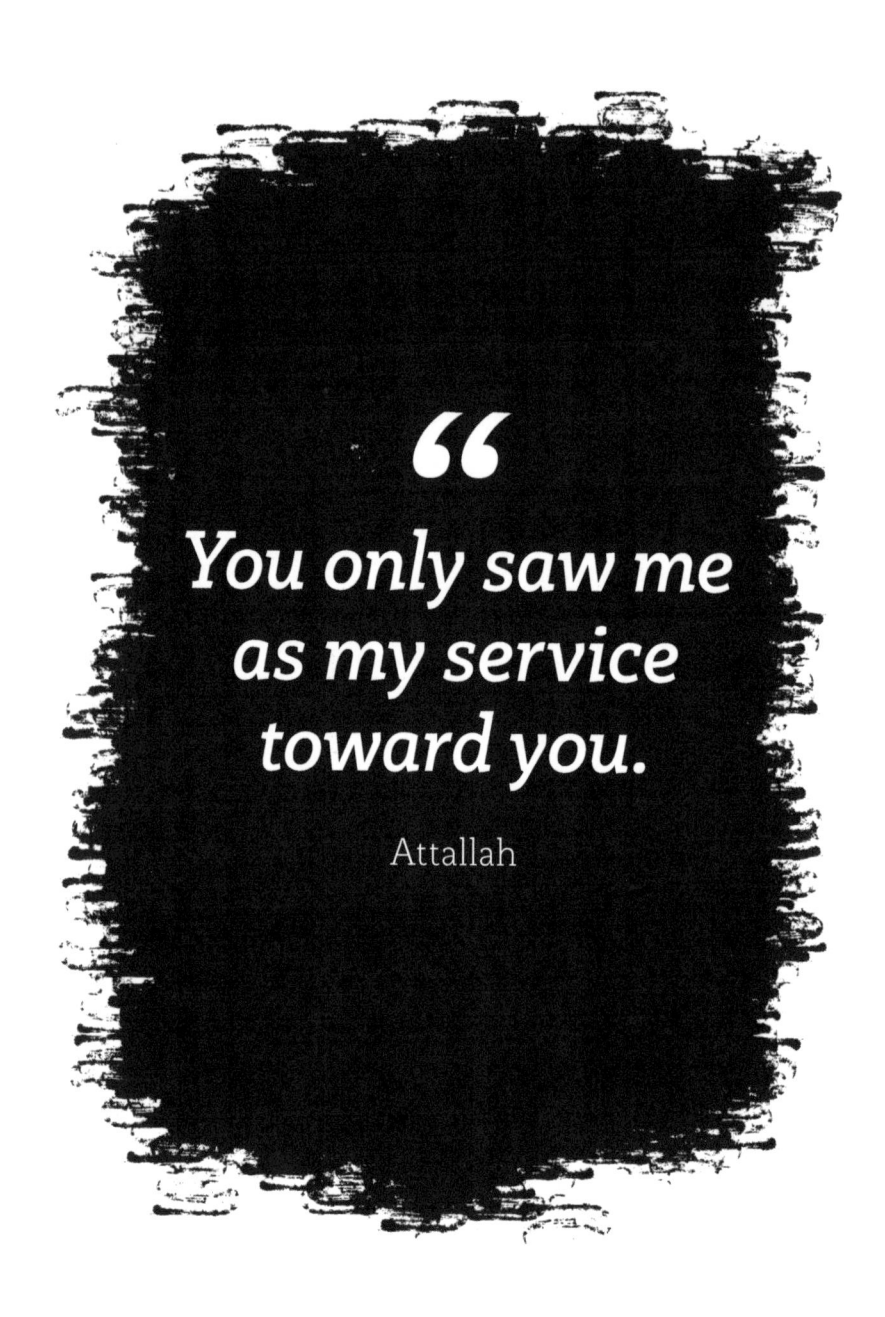

— Attallah

FUELED BY LOVE
Carrie

Dear Black Woman,

Your past, present, and future matter to me. Your voice deserves to be heard. Your stories deserve to be believed. Your safety and wellness deserve to be valued. Your ideas deserve to be given life. Your presence deserves to be respected and recognized. You deserve to lead, love, and exist just as you are.

From my heart to your heart please know I'm here for the **revolution** that leads to repair and reconciliation.

I am fueled by love, inspired by hope, and willing to take the risks. I am here to listen and learn. I am an accomplice in this necessary work. I am here to end racism and do the "heart" work. I am here for the long journey by confronting the past and embracing our future.

I am showing up!

Appreciatively,
Carrie

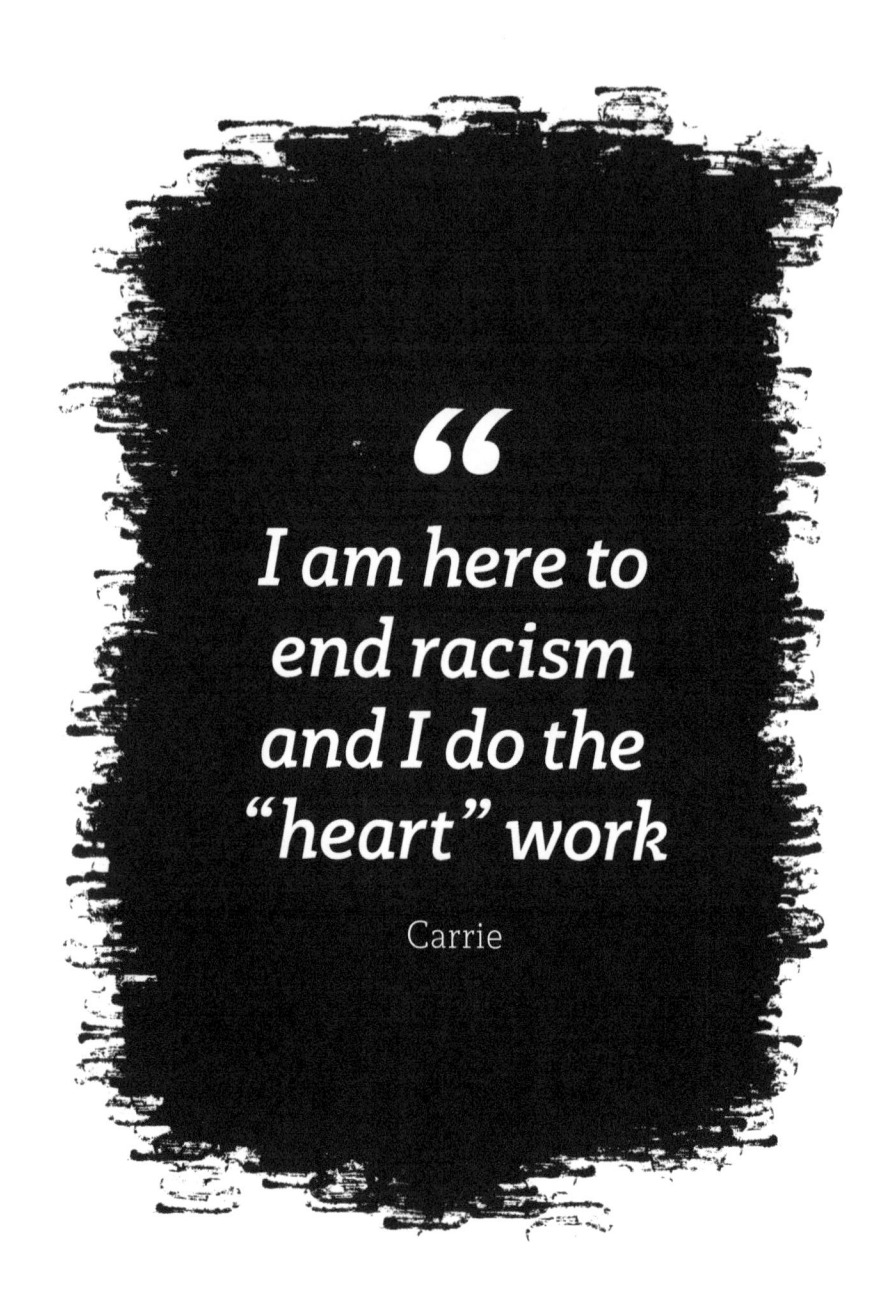

> *I am here to end racism and I do the "heart" work*
>
> Carrie

CELEBRATING WITHOUT APOLOGY

Sheila

Dear White Woman,

It took me years – decades, really – to appreciate the fullness of who I am as a Black woman. I wasn't born knowing it. I wasn't raised to embrace it. In fact, for much of my life, I was disconnected from the beauty, the power, and the history that runs through my veins. I had to learn to assimilate, to fit into a world that wasn't built for me or people like me. I was told, subtly and sometimes not-so-subtly, that the way to survive, to thrive even, was to suppress my Blackness and adapt to the predominantly White culture around me.

I vividly remember a time when my boyfriend told me he liked me because I was Black but acted White. At the time, I took it as a compliment, even though deep down, it felt like a dagger to my soul. *What was he really saying? What was he saying about the other women who looked like me and didn't "act White"?* I didn't fully grasp what he was really saying or how damaging those words were to my sense of self. Looking back, I realize how disconnected I was from my own identity. Growing up, there weren't many Black faces in the media or history books. Representation was scarce, and when it did appear, it was a moment of awe. I remember my parents excitedly calling my sisters and me to the TV whenever Black performers like the Jackson 5 or the Supremes were on. We would sit, mesmerized, because, for those few moments, we felt seen.

But that was the exception, not the rule. My parents had moved from the South, determined to give their daughters a better life than the segregated world they had grown up in. The focus was on getting a good education and going to college, not so much on nurturing a love and appreciation of our culture. They, too, were trying to adapt the best way they knew how in a society that constantly reminded them of their place. Education was supposed to be our ticket to opportunity, to something better. But education couldn't shield me from the racism I encountered.

I remember standing in the lunch line one day at school with two of my White friends. One of them got bumped into by another student, and when asked what happened, she replied, "Oh, a nigger ran into me." I was stunned–hurt in a way that I didn't know how to process. I had no tools to confront that kind of hate. I just swallowed the pain, because relationships were important to me. I didn't want conflict. So, I ignored it and told myself to push past it.

But the cost of doing that was high. In trying to make peace, I lost myself. I rejected the very essence of who I am. I became a friend to everyone but an enemy of my own identity.

It wasn't until I left my hometown for college that I began to truly embrace my Blackness. I joined a Black sorority and became part of a progressive, non-denominational church that celebrated the Black presence in the Bible. Later, I moved to Atlanta, and surrounded myself with strong, beautiful Black people who knew exactly who they were and embraced their identity and purpose with pride. These experiences awakened something profound in me: I matter. I realized I didn't need to adapt to Whiteness to be seen or valued. I could stand fully in my Blackness and be proud.

You might wonder why I now hold so tightly to my Blackness, and why I dedicate my energy to serving Black women. It's because I spent too many years disconnected from that part of myself. And now, I can't let it go. I won't. I love my people, and I love myself. I finally understand that I don't need permission to be Black and proud. I can celebrate who I am, without apology. And that's exactly what I do every day.

I want you to understand something. For many of us, racism isn't just a word or a political issue – it's a lived experience. White privilege is real, even if it's invisible to you. It's the luxury of not having to think about race every single day. It's the freedom to exist in a world that caters to you, that affirms you, that uplifts you, while quietly telling me that I don't belong unless I conform. I spent too much of my life trying to conform, trying to be acceptable in a world that often saw my Blackness as a threat or a defect.

I share this not to blame you, but to invite you into a deeper understanding. I hope this letter makes you pause and reflect on what it means to exist in a world where White privilege is the default setting. I hope it helps you see the cost that racism exacts on Black lives–not just in blatant acts of violence but in the everyday erasures, the silencing, and the invisibility.

DEAR WHITE WOMAN, DEAR BLACK WOMAN

I spent years closing my eyes to this truth in an effort to keep the peace. But peace without justice is a lie. If we are ever to heal, if we are ever to move forward, we must confront the truth. Not with anger, but with love.

I hope you will join me in this.

With love and honesty,
Sheila
National Harbor, Maryland

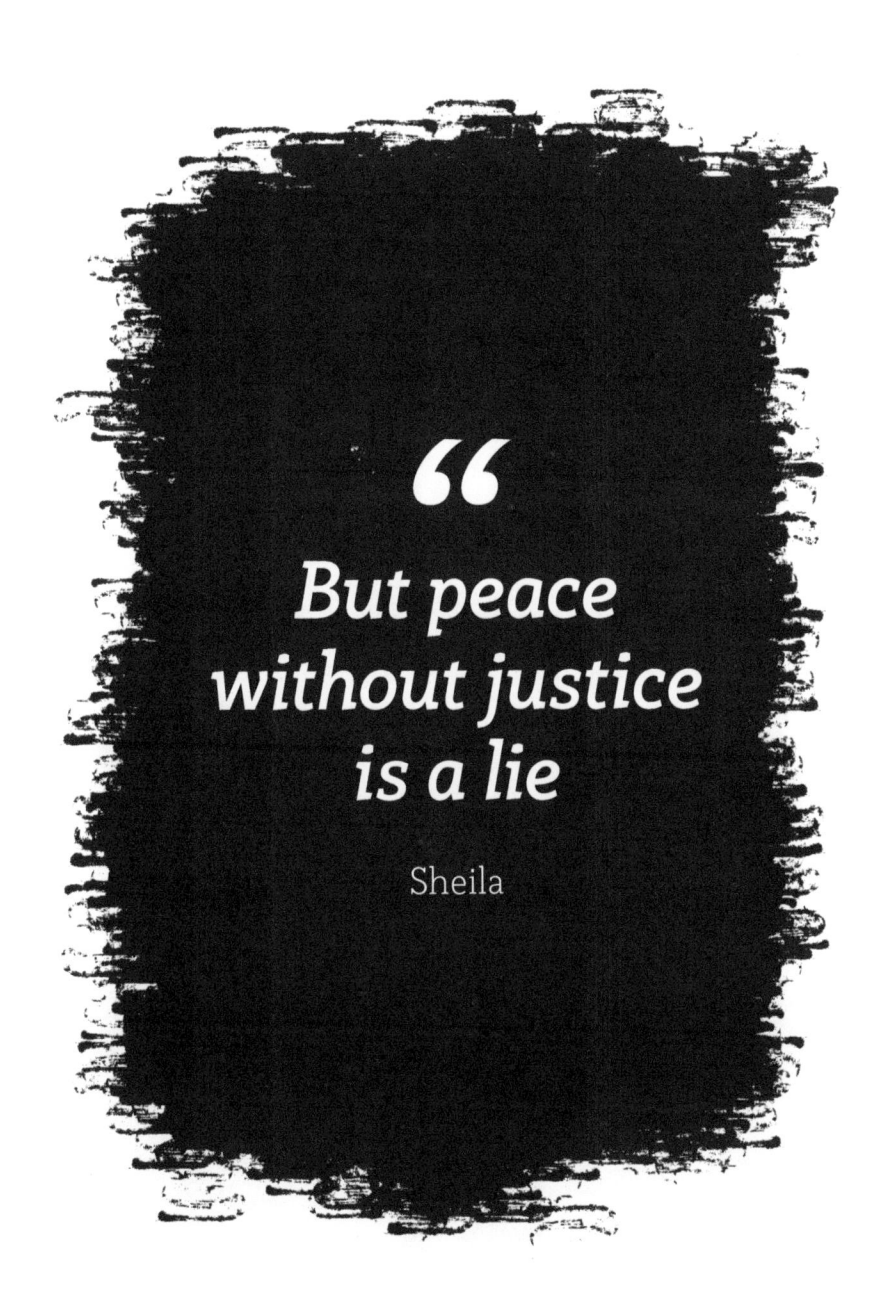

> **But peace without justice is a lie**
>
> Sheila

WHITE WOMAN'S TEARS

Lisa

Dear Black Woman,

The following poem emerges from a lifelong grief over love and friendship lost, sliced by countless papercuts from a racist culture that despises all women. Let me share with you an early memory, one that still haunts me. I attended Crawford County Elementary School, and in the first grade, I made a friend. She was smart, bookish, and quiet–much like me. We could talk about anything. We would sit together in the high school bleachers, sharing the day's news like only six-year-old girls can. But almost as soon as we found each other, the whispering began.

At first, the words seemed insignificant, but they hung in the air, heavy like poison gas. Words like, "Are you allowed to play at her house?" Words like, "You two shouldn't sit together." Words like, "Why are you friends with her?" These comments came from all directions. Even at six, I was perceptive enough to recognize the racism. But I was more focused on being a "good girl," burdened by the expectations of those around me. I felt the weight of authority from my parents, my pastor, deacons, revival ministers, missionaries who slept on our couches, and, of course, my teachers. In that small evangelical town, where God, your father, your pastor, angels, demons, and deacons were all interested in the behavior of little girls, it felt like even my thoughts were monitored lest I slip up and slide into Hell.

In this oppressive atmosphere, I barely noticed that I was sitting next to my friend less and less. Eventually, we drifted apart, and by the time I was seven, she was gone from my life. I still miss her. I mourn what could have been – the blossoming of our innocent childhood friendship, the pure joy of talking about bugs and butterflies without the weight of adult prejudice.

I vividly remember one of our last conversations, where we tried to make sense of what was happening. We put our arms next to each other on the bleachers, and they didn't seem so different. If you looked closely, mine was pinker, and hers was tanner. We giggled as we compared ourselves to a chicken–white meat and dark meat. We both preferred thighs and drumsticks, which was what we usually got as kids anyway. But to us, it was clear: we were one chicken, one whole, even if the world tried to cut us into parts.

White Women's Tears

White women were coddled,
while Black women were hobbled,
This is how evil was complicitly accomplished
and our connection as women broken and tarnished.

Weak is what happens when you aren't allowed sport,
are systematically barred from the social court...
Withering year after year, hungry in body, mind and soul
the voice in your head is not in your control.

Thus fear is how they mastered us.

DEAR WHITE WOMAN, DEAR BLACK WOMAN

Fear, watered with a small appreciation,
Applied poisonly and precisely,
where it chokes sanity,
as if our strength's peak
were protecting our men
from being weak.

Fear lays a sticky foundation
For the further destruction of trust,
Because, little girl, be afraid of us.
Men who aren't family are rotten as pus.
You can't be strong like your brothers,
And you aren't allowed to cuss.

What could you say anyway?
Not educated in the real world–business and violence–
What irrelevant thoughts you have are best
suffered in silence.
Shut in "for protection" and "shut out" for security,
Your future devolves in shepherded obscurity.

Here is where we speak of White women's tears.
No one wants our tears, us pink, pampered things.
Don't ruin your mascara. Why do you cling?
If you don't stop sniffling, I'll give you something to cry about.
Stop making it about you, that's how the inner voice rings.

Haven't you learned it's never about you?
But that's not true. That's the lie some men hope we believe.

It is about you. It's about me and you.
With the first triple beat of mind, heart and gut in sync–
there flows a consequential drop of what's due
That this-is-wrong essence, it's actually you,

WHITE WOMAN'S TEARS

maybe the first you, you ever knew.
These tears soften the manacles that bind the mind.
Tears quicken the blood that fear dried over time.
Tears bear bodily witness to all that's wrong.
Tears signal there are better ways to belong.

Tears irrigate our insides, from fearing to feeling.
When we first feel ourselves, we find we're grieving.
After we've grieved, if we get that luck,
We build a new personality, and have a lot to shuck.

Black women, White women, all women are now my wings. The cultural change we embody together is made of ancestors' dreams. United, we are more than enough to conquer individual fears and cultural leers. Unity is the wholehearted change that truly dries our tears.

———

With grief and love,
Lisa

> **Unity is the wholehearted change that truly dries our tears.**
>
> Lisa

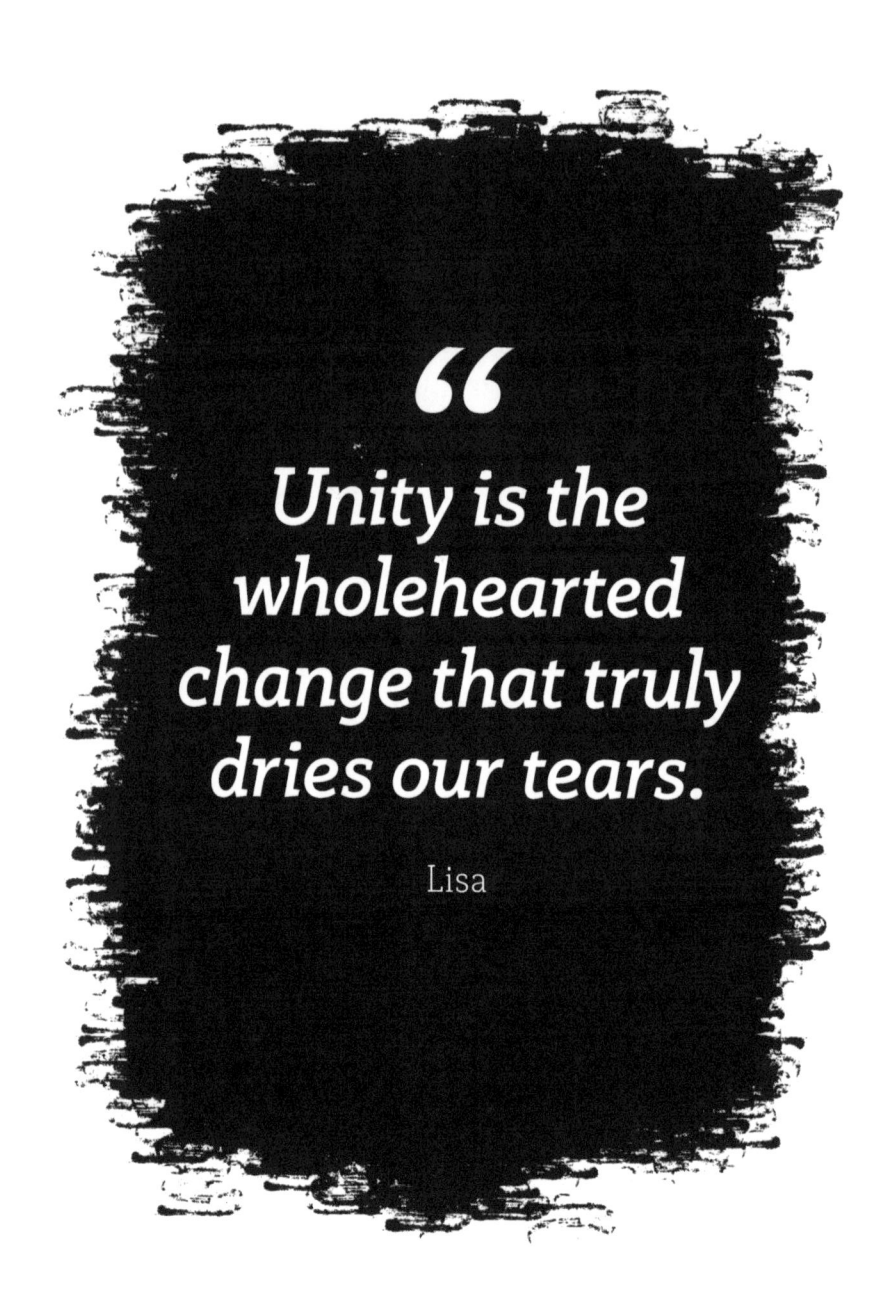

HEAL THE SUFFERING

Audrey

Dear White Woman,

I'm writing this letter to you to share my observations from years; with your permission, I would start with this scenario: Without going too far back in history, I'm identifying how I saw some White women wanting Black men for their gain and not thinking about having biracial children with the Black man. My purpose is to hope that more women would consider the children's feelings about being mixed. Women, to me the Black men are looking for opportunities to get ahead, not bring biracial children into this world. I share this observation with my family. I have seen and heard of children who are hidden, not claimed, abused, and heartbroken, without understanding of why they were even born. Studies show that it can be difficult to raise a biracial child as they deal with racism and microaggressions. Biracial children may have to navigate a racial identity different from their parents.

Mental health practitioners need to be aware of their biases and practice with cultural humility. Just reference Psychology Today. All my life I was aware that my cousins had a White Mother and my uncle was Black, but as a child, it did not matter. I didn't see color; I just saw people. However, once I matured and connected with my cousins, they shared and showed their disturbing childhood life stories. I begin to think Why would a White woman, put their children through that kind of pain? The world is suffering enough! One related area of racial identity that has been neglected by counseling researchers is the study of racial identity development in biracial children.

Dear White women, my request for you is to gain more understanding of the responsibilities that come with raising biracial children in a world that can be challenging for them, not so much you having a Black man. The staring of mixed children continues, and the pain continues. My biracial female cousin tried to hide her color and her children's race by marrying a White man and encouraging her children to do the same. I guess that worked for her at one time; however, she suffers from not claiming her Father, while her White Mother is heartbroken that her Black man continues pursuing his God-given assignment and was hardly home with the family they created together. White women who want a Black man: think about the messages, purposes, exceptions, and bitterness for yourself and your children's desires. Your reflections on your family's experiences highlight the emotional struggles that biracial children can face, including issues of identity, belonging, and the effects of racism and microaggressions. It's crucial to consider how these factors impact their mental health and well-being. My call is for greater awareness among mental health practitioners regarding the unique challenges faced by biracial children.

Understanding cultural nuances and biases can foster more effective support for these children and their families. White women, my personal experiences with my cousins also underscore the importance of empathy and the need for White women to thoughtfully consider the implications of their relationships and the environments they create for their children.

I kindly ask for your consideration of all that I have shared in hopes of expanding the discussion and perhaps even healing.

Thanks,
Audrey

> **The world is suffering enough!**
>
> Audrey

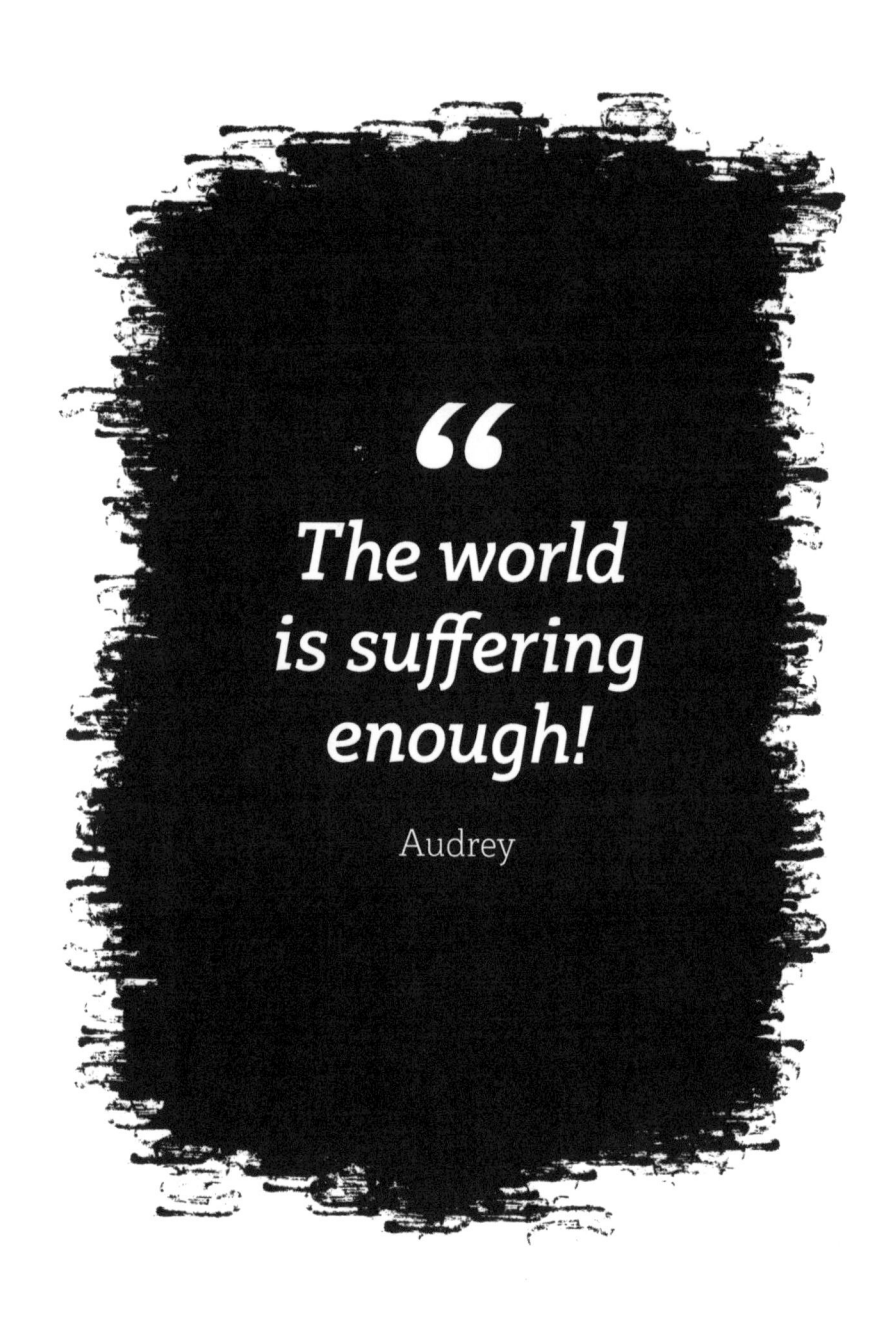

DOING THE WORK

Heather

Dear Black Woman,

I know my words mean nothing and my actions mean everything. My words are backed by action, and though it may not always be the right action, I am dedicated to continuous learning, self-reflection, and sitting in the inevitable discomfort that will come when I do get things wrong.

I want to start by acknowledging that as humans we are inherently self-centered. I know I am. See, I did it! I do realize that it isn't all about me. That said, today, in this letter, I plan to share some of my thoughts, feelings, and experiences in hopes that this communication will be healing for both of us and bring us closer.

I am embarrassed to admit that I didn't start really doing race work until 2020 after George Floyd was murdered. His story, that video, and his cries for his mom impacted me profoundly. We both know it wasn't the first and it wouldn't be the last time we would see this type of footage. I think that because we were all home due to the pandemic, we were forced to actually face it, feel it, and deal with it, more so than when we were all living our normal, busy lives. Pre-pandemic, there were days and even weeks where I wouldn't have time to watch the news because I would be busy driving to school, to work, working, doing pickup, making dinner, then more work, maybe a few minutes of a show, then bed, and repeat. When George Floyd was murdered, I watched the news for hours, I was immersed in it. I think so many people were. I remember the exact moment when I heard about it. I looked over and my wife was on her computer and she started crying. When I asked her what happened, she told me and showed me the news footage. It's a memory I'll never forget.

Growing up, I naively thought things were getting better. I grew up in Miami, which is very culturally diverse, and then I moved to Atlanta which I think is almost equally culturally diverse, but I think even more connected and community-oriented – which is why I've stayed here. When I dove into the work, I realized how wrong I was about things being better and over the next several years as I dove deeper, things were taking a turn and actually getting worse. Sadly, I see that many companies are cutting their DEI teams, and people are back to living their busy lives. It feels like we've gone backward. I am one of the people who has been pulled back into a busy life, but I couldn't look at myself in the mirror if I didn't continue doing this work.

For me, doing the work means consuming information from reputable sources to become more knowledgeable about the past, present, and taking steps to help shape the future I hope to see for all of us. It's taking ownership of how I've contributed to an intentionally designed system of injustice and realizing that it is something I have benefited from. It is using the knowledge and awareness I've gained to make choices that align with my beliefs, even when it makes things harder for me, because it's the right thing to do. It's about speaking up and taking a stand when it's uncomfortable and even dangerous.

I will continue to make mistakes, but I will also continue doing the work. I will be authentic, self aware and I will do my best to listen and be empathetic. The depth of this is overwhelming. It is ingrained in both of us at a cellular level whether we like it or not. I acknowledge that and hope to be a part of the incremental change that shifts the cellular patterns, shaping a future of love.

Thank you for reading my words, and I hope you feel my action, which in this moment would consist of a hug if you would receive one.

Yours,
Heather

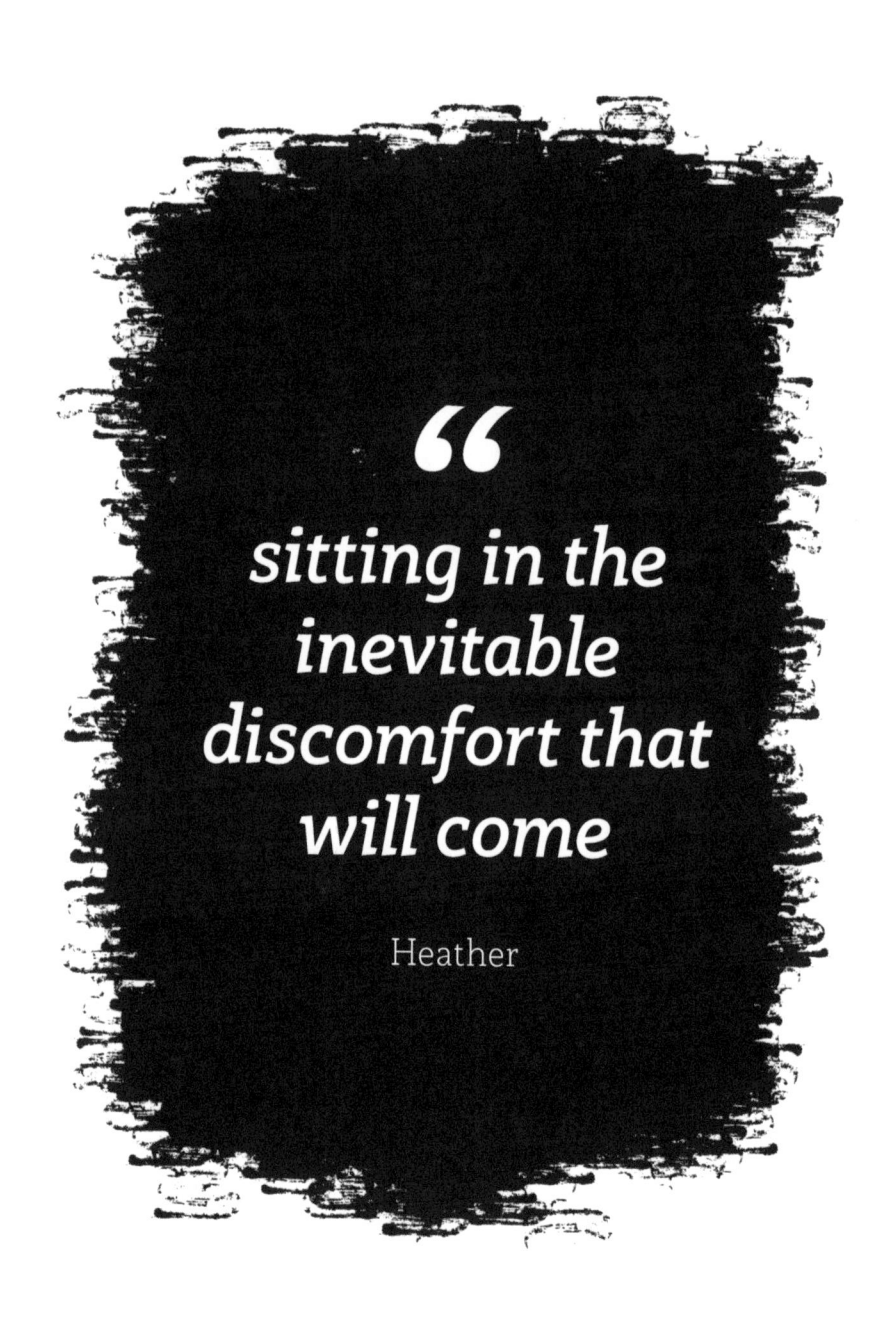

> *sitting in the inevitable discomfort that will come*
>
> Heather

WHAT ALLYSHIP DEMANDS

Taylor

Dear White Woman,

My name is Taylor and I am a Black woman. I am writing to share with you today an important truth: allyship is not a simple statement or an acknowledgment of the suffering and hardships of another group. It requires a continuous process of reflection, education, communication, and action. These are also the necessary components of a genuine apology, as allyship and accountability go hand in hand.

Now let me tell you *why* I'm writing about apologies.

At the end of January 2021, I was listening to my at-the-time favorite podcast, *99% Invisible*. *99% Invisible* is a radio show about design and architecture and how things came to be. On this particular day, I played the "Articles of Interest #5: Blue Jeans" episode as I drove my father through my South Carolina hometown, excited to have him listen to one of my favorite quarantine discoveries. Here's an excerpt from the transcript:

> Guest, Lukaza Branfman-Verissimo: I*ndigo had first been cultivated in the US in the 1740s by a woman... Eliza Pinkney. Born in Antigua... her family then had plantations in South*

Carolina and she and her family moved there. Her father had sent her some indigo seeds from the Caribbean. And she thought, "Hmmm let's try this!" and she was able to cultivate enough indigo to make it a cash crop.

Producer, White Woman, Avery Trufelman: *In that way, American indigo has a cool, feminist success story!*

Let me repeat that for you. The producer of this episode, Avery Trufelman, lauded Eliza Pickney's cultivation of indigo, which was the fruit of labor forced from the brutally enslaved, as a "feminist success." When I heard her say this, my stomach **plummeted.** I could not believe my ears. There I was, a Black woman from South Carolina, listening to a White woman erase the subjugation of my ancestors and "#girlboss" it up.

I reached out to Avery and the podcast on Twitter to get some answers about how this could have ever been published. This is what brings us to apologies. Avery did respond to my request for comment. However, I privately contextualized why the statement is violent, and what I got in return was absolution, deflection, and no acknowledgment from 99% Invisible, which she no longer works for.

I write this letter now with the hope that a conversation regarding apologies can lead to greater understanding and reparations between us sisters. In order to discuss what a substantial apology includes, I believe that it is necessary to acknowledge White fragility and victimization, because the components of a substantive apology are particularly important when the apology is coming from a person of privilege. In plain speak: White sisters, y'all have a habit of being violent or just offensive and running from that harm – which you have the ability to do because you are White.

WHAT ALLYSHIP DEMANDS

How many times have we seen a screenshot of a Notes app that more or less states:

I didn't mean to hurt anyone. I didn't know any better. I'm sorry if you were offended.

These shallow apologies fail to show accountability. They fail to acknowledge the root causes of the wrongdoing. They fail to address the impact the action had on individuals or communities. So, let's close the Notes app and discuss what comes with a real apology.

My concept of a substantive apology relates to the theory of restorative justice. Rather than focusing on penal punishments, whether that is a prison sentence or a ban on social media, restorative justice brings the individuals involved together with the purpose of repairing the harm done to the victims and the larger community with the purpose of reintegrating all parties back into the community. You do not place the emotional labor that comes with the process of accountability on members of the group(s) you are apologizing to. You do open channels of communication to see what form of accountability is expected by the harmed community. And then you get your hands dirty and do the work of being better. This is what I expect of your allyship: moving past fragility and performative activism into the work needed to exist in community with your Black sisters.

Warmly,
Taylor

> **allyship and accountability go hand in hand**
>
> Taylor

A COMMITMENT

Gina

Dear Black Woman,

Thank you. First and foremost, I want to express my gratitude.

I am curious to know how much gratitude you have received in your lifetime. Does this even matter when our structures and systems have imposed so many obstacles on your life? Even though these systems pre-date our births, I am committed to standing up and being an advocate to dismantle systemic racism and reimagine how equanimity will serve you and all women collectively.

As a child, my White body did not comprehend the challenges you faced while we were playing double-dutch on the streets in South Minneapolis. I have memories of peace and belonging, do you?

Fast forward forty years later, and those same streets are now the murder scene of George Floyd. I'm waking up and seeing your reality. Yes, I know it has taken a long time. I am now ready, more than ever, to come alongside you. We need all women to stand up, link arms, and unite as ***"Survivors of the Status Quo."***

As a White woman, I am committed to and hope to inspire my White sisters to:

1. Come to the table prepared to give our full **attention.** We aspire to be a safe place to share your heartaches and hold collective trauma. We will be honest about our White fragility and not use tears as manipulation.

2. Do the work! We will be curious and vulnerable. We will leverage available resources and not ask you to educate us. We will have a level of **care** for you that will deepen our bond. We will love you so profoundly that it will set a new standard of friendship and partnership.

3. Honor the good you do. We will notice what you do, lift you up, and celebrate you! We will see the similarities and differences and know we are stronger together because of our unique qualities. We will not judge you, as we have barely begun to get to know you. We will be open to supporting you in the ways you desire. We will also be open to feedback when we get it wrong (which we will).

Yes, these are only words on a page; however, I must also be intentional with my actions. I am committed to continual education, self-reflection, and making changes to be your co-creator in reimagining a world where you are seen, valued, and heard. My friends and I actively support and purchase from Black women-owned businesses; we listen deeply to Black women authors, poets, and work in the community supporting Black entrepreneurs. As a human resources professional, I work with numerous companies that are concerned about hiring processes and pay inequities. Most importantly, change starts from the top, and I was thrilled to vote for a Black woman as President of The United States of America in 2024.

A COMMITMENT

I declare it is not acceptable for me to be ignorant. I admit I have been a part of the problem. That is hard to say, and it is more accurate than false. Please know that the depth of my soul has been triggered, and my glasses are cleaner and less rose-colored. I will not sit still and look pretty! I will not allow my sisters to sit in pain alone. I embrace empathy, and I am here for you. You are valued.

As White and Black women, we can demonstrate pure love and provide a new level of consciousness for the next generation. What beauty can we create in the world through one conversation with a Black woman, one relationship with a Black woman, and one letter to a Black woman? I'm excited about the possibilities!

With excitement for the possibilities,
Gina

> "What beauty can we create in the world through one conversation

Gina

AFTERWORD

Dear White Woman... Dear Black Woman...

This is us... this is our tapestry.

Let us not view this book as merely a collection of letters; it is the inception of a movement and a pathway to our collective healing. We embarked on this profound and transformative journey with the hope of bringing healing to the soul of a nation. Fifty-six women answered the call: Black Women agreed to write letters to White Women and White Women agreed to write letters to Black Women. Together, we delved into the intricate complexities of life, dealing with race, identity, relationships, and the interwoven threads of our shared humanity that bind us all. Within the pages of *Dear White Woman, Dear Black Woman*, we dared to share our truths and be courageously vulnerable. Each letter represented a seed of hope and a clarion call to embrace other-centeredness. Through these masterfully woven threads of truth, perspectives, and experiences, we have opened doors to deeper innerstanding, compassion, forgiveness, and healing.

Greater than one moment

As I pen these words in the aftermath of the United States 2024 Presidential election, our nation stands at a pivotal crossroads. The election's outcome has laid bare the duality of our national conscience, leaving many feeling as though their fervent pleas have gone unheard by the Creator of the universe, while others believe their prayers have been both heard and answered. In this juxtaposition, we find ourselves in a space where disappointment and joy coexist, crafting a landscape of deep-seated tension and complexity.

At my core, I am an optimist, yet there is a cry in my soul as the election has once again illuminated the deep political, racial, and economic divides intertwined into the fabric of our nation. The polarization and division among family members, communities, and friends weigh heavily on my heart. Despite these ongoing challenges and the multidimensional layers of emotions, I choose to rise above the cultural distractions and noise. I embrace my faith and yield my soul to the steadfast hope that dwells within me.

I am hopeful because as a people, I know we are greater than any one moment. I am hopeful because as women, we possess an immense power to shift atmospheres and in the midst of chaotic times, we find a way to lean into the realm of possibilities and align with our inner strength. Yes, we cry...we hurt...and we even get tired along the way, but our inherent ability to innovate and persevere in the face of challenges, adversity, heartbreak, and setbacks is nothing short of extraordinary.

So, where do we go from here?

When we find ourselves facing uncertainty and fear, we must remember that our strength lies in our ability to listen, to empathize, and to unite. Though it is challenging, we must commit to elevating our consciousness beyond self-interest and embrace our shared humanity. This means the ability to embrace individuals we do not agree with or look like. By aligning with a love-centered consciousness, we can begin to heal and transform our world.

AFTERWORD

These letters are just one way to lay the foundation and get the dialogue started. And while I recognize that a compilation of letters alone cannot dismantle unjust systems, it can indeed serve as a powerful catalyst for change. There is critical work to be done, and we need each other. As women, we must remember never to underestimate the influence of our united voices and the incredible impact of our shared stories. By choosing to be upstanders and speaking out against injustice, we can create a ripple effect that challenges and transforms the unjust structures that divide us.

The composers of these letters leaned into their truths and dared to be uncomfortably courageous. These letters remind us that every voice matters and that through empathy, understanding, and united effort, we can begin to address and transform the inequities that continue to persist in our world house. These letters stand as a testament to our universal human experience and a clarion call to action, urging us to engage in honest and courageous dialogue. We can no longer run from our past. We must acknowledge it, embrace it, and move forward with a deeper commitment to love and honor humanity.

It's possible. . .

What does it look like to become a nation's soul and healing? It is possible, but it's not a journey for the faint of heart. It requires our collective will, unconditional love for all people, intentionality, and unwavering commitment to transform unjust systems and make room for all God's children.

The *Dear White Woman, Dear Black Woman* book project began with Black women and White women to address the deep-rooted racial divide that has shaped our society for generations.

As women in one nation, we have lived parallel lives, often separated by systemic racism and societal barriers. By starting with Black and White women, we can directly confront the historical wounds that have kept us apart and created many layers of pain, distrust, and misunderstandings. This project is not just about acknowledging past injustices; it's about building a future where all women can stand together in solidarity and support.

The ultimate goal is to dismantle all the "isms" that separate us and create a healthy foundation and space for all women, regardless of race – a space where everyone can listen, learn, and grow together. Let us commit to continuing this open-hearted dialogue and creating a beautiful tapestry woven with threads of transparency, truth, and love. Let us continue to create and share in safe spaces to build bridges of understanding and forgiveness. In this urgent and critical hour, let us answer the call to protect the future of our children by creating a world where love prevails.

Dear White Woman... Dear Black Woman...
It is possible to become and heal the soul of a nation.

ACKNOWLEDGMENTS

The journey of creating *Dear White Woman, Dear Black Woman: A Tapestry of Letters for Hope and Healing* has been a divinely inspired and orchestrated endeavor. I recognize that I am merely a steward of this project, and for that, I am profoundly grateful.

I wish to express my deepest gratitude to my Creator for entrusting me with this mission. This work transcends my individual efforts; it is a response to a higher calling to contribute to the greater good. Throughout this journey, I have often found myself in awe, intensely honored to be chosen as the vessel for this vision and to witness its realization. My heartfelt prayer is that this work fulfills its purpose–to bridge divides and bring hope and healing to the soul of our nation.

The evolution of this project has been a profound and transformative experience, one that would not have been possible without the support and contributions of many remarkable women – some I know and others I have never met. These courageous women answered the call and understood the urgent need for women to take the lead in bridging the divides. I am deeply honored and intensely grateful to each woman for contributing her voices, perspectives, and experiences to this project. Because of the collective courage, honesty, and compassion, we have woven a powerful tapestry that will inspire and heal.

I am especially grateful to Jenn Graham, Monique Rochon, Vonnetta L. West, and Angela Oxford for believing in this project and investing their time and energy into its realization. This book started with many Saturday morning Zoom meetings. Their faith in this vision has been a cornerstone of its manifestation and realization. This book is a testament to the power of collaboration, vulnerability, faith, and hope. Together, we have created something truly extraordinary – a beautiful tapestry laced with threads of hope, healing, and love, and for that, I am grateful.

I must extend my heartfelt gratitude to Jenn Graham. Every so often, you encounter someone who becomes just as excited about your dreams as you are. For me, that person is Jenn. Her unwavering dedication, commitment, and belief in this project have been nothing short of inspiring. When the project began to lose momentum and I got caught up in the busyness of life, Jenn sent me a friendly email to remind me that "now is the time." She introduced me to the incredible Ripples Media team, and the rest, as they say, is history. All I can say is. . . I'm grateful that our chance meeting at a conference didn't end after just one conversation. Jenn worked tirelessly encouraging White women to participate in this project. The accountability, enthusiasm, and excitement Jenn brought to this project have been unparalleled. I am beyond thankful for her friendship and unwavering support.

I also extend my heartfelt thanks to the incredible team at Ripples Media: Andrew, Nicole, Dorothy, and the entire Ripples team. This team ROCKS! Their patience and understanding of a writer's processing style are truly inspiring. We set an ambitious timeline, and despite my occasional delays, the Ripples team's kindness and professionalism made this journey an extraordinary experience. I am immensely grateful for the meticulous care given to the cover design. A special thank you to the cover designer, Burtch Hunter, for capturing my vision

ACKNOWLEDGMENTS

and working tirelessly until it was perfect. I have a saying, "The energy you put in is what people will experience." I have never worked with a team where the energy was so consistently empowering and encouraging. If my theory holds true, everyone who reads this book will be tremendously blessed because the Ripples team's energy is phenomenal.

I must acknowledge my incredible family and friends. I am blessed with an amazing village whose encouragement has been unparalleled. When I shared this project with them, I received so much encouragement. One thing is certain: when you share your dreams with them, you must see them through, because they are like children in the back seat of a car, anxiously awaiting their arrival at the destination. Their occasional, "Are we there yet?" serves as a reminder of their eager anticipation for the manifestation of your dream. I am profoundly grateful for their excitement, faith, and love.

Thank you to every woman who embraces this work and joins us on this journey.

Thank you, thank you, thank you!

Ubuntu... I am because you are.
Bonita T. Hampton Smith

ABOUT THE AUTHOR & CONTRIBUTORS

Bonita T. Hampton Smith

Bonita T. Hampton Smith is a visionary leader whose life's work has been dedicated to uplifting women, inspiring leaders, and transforming lives. As an inspirational speaker, certified nonviolence trainer, businesswoman, and author, Bonita's journey is a powerful testament to her unwavering commitment to making a difference.

Her literary journey began with the heartfelt collection of poetry, "Echoes of My Soul," published in 2003. This was followed by her enchanting children's book, "Linzy Binzy, Around the World with Friends – First Adventure: Loving the Skin We're In," inspired by her niece, Lindsey Elizabeth Hampton. This book aims to nurture self-love and inspire children to embrace their inner brilliance.

Bonita's passion for empowering women is the cornerstone of her mission. As a former Chaplain, she dedicated herself to supporting and empowering incarcerated women, women addicted to substance abuse and those on federal assistance, helping them transition to self-sufficiency. Her dedication to helping women discover their true selves and live out their highest potential is exemplified in her "Dear White Woman, Dear Black Woman" project, which fosters understanding, healing and unity among women of diverse backgrounds.

Bonita is the President of BHS Consulting, LLC, a company dedicated to "Bringing Healthy Solutions" to nonprofits with a focus on strategizing for impact and results and leading "inside-out." Currently serving as the Chief Operations Officer for the Martin Luther King, Jr. Center for Nonviolent Social Change, Bonita continues to drive positive change.

"My deepest aspiration is to be a vessel of unconditional love, radiant light, and infectious laughter. Love that embraces without conditions, light that dispels darkness and fear, and laughter that brings joy and a smile to every heart I encounter."

ABOUT THE AUTHOR & CONTRIBUTORS

Jenn Graham

Jenn Graham is the founder and CEO of Inclusivv, a culture transformation company helping leaders build trust, belonging and inclusion through structured conversations. As a social innovation designer and former TEDxAtlanta organizer, Jenn has pioneered a unique approach to social change, using the power of structured conversations to bring together diverse voices and perspectives. Jenn speaks and consults, inspiring others to harness the power of conversation to bridge divides, foster understanding, and build stronger, more connected communities. In 2022, Inclusivv was a finalist in the SHRM 2022 Better Workplaces Challenge Cup, a global competition among startups working to build better workplaces, and a better world. Jenn Graham has been featured as a "2020 World-Changing Woman in Conscious Business" by Conscious Media Company, and recognized by the Atlanta Business Chronicle as "Small Business Person of the Year - Rising Star" in 2019.

Vonnetta L. West

Vonnetta L. West is a cultural consultant, leadership strategist, nonviolence educator, and learning experience curator known for her subject knowledge and trainings in the areas of social justice, civic engagement, and community building. Vonnetta is also a speaker and facilitator, often working with organizations to promote a culture of honor, inspired leadership, and courageous, hopeful engagement. Her work emphasizes the power of empathy, active listening, and strategic collaboration to foster stronger, more compassionate individuals, organizations, and communities. Vonnetta is the founder and CEO of Go West Consulting LLC and the pastor of Our Neighbor's House, which is building an Educational Center in Liberia, West Africa.

Monique Rochon

Monique Rochon is an educator, intuitive paper artist and penpal. She is originally from Bloomfield, Connecticut and comes from a family with Louisiana roots. She is an alumnus of Howard University where she graduated with a Bachelor of Arts in Administration of Justice and Political Science. Monique spent 10 years of her professional career in The District of Columbia, which remains formative in her understanding of Blackness in communities and geographies. Monique later obtained her Masters degree in Education with a focus in Curriculum and Instruction from the University of South Florida. She has worked as a classroom teacher in the K-12 system in both Washington, D.C. and New Orleans, Louisiana. She currently serves adult learners in the Higher Education space to navigate the intricacies of their collegiate journeys. In her free time, Monique enjoys weight training, reading, visiting local coffee shops and spending time with her Yorkie named Nola.

Angela Oxford

Angela Oxford is the Senior Manager on the Community Resilience Team for the Walmart Foundation she serves the Northwest Arkansas Region. Formerly, Angela served as the founding director of the Center for Community Engagement of the University of Arkansas for fourteen years. She also served as Program Director for Big Brothers Big Sisters NWA and Associate Director of Corporate Partnerships for Hands On Atlanta. She has a B.S. in Education from Arkansas State University and a Master of Divinity from Southern Baptist Theological Seminary. She is completing her dissertation for her doctorate from the University of Arkansas in Higher Education. She is from Northwest Arkansas, and she is mom to Jack and Ella Fei.

REFLECTION & DISCUSSION

―

Personal Reflection

Welcome to the personal reflection section of *Dear White Woman, Dear Black Woman*. This part of the book is designed to help you delve deeper into your own thoughts, feelings, and experiences as you reflect on the letters and stories you have read.

The hope is that these questions will take you on a deeper journey of self-discovery, empathy, and even forgiveness and healing (if necessary). As you ponder each question, please take your time to explore your inner landscape and consider how the words from your White sister and Black sister resonate within your soul.

Remember, there are no right or wrong answers–only your unique perspective and insights. Embrace this opportunity to connect with your true self, challenge your assumptions, and envision how you can contribute to a more understanding and bridging the divide in our world.

The healing starts with our innerstanding of ourselves and others. To ensure you are able to find a space for honest introspection and meaningful contemplation, I suggest finding your own place of solace as you journey within. Let's do the work and let's be intentional about healing ourselves, our communities, our nation and our world. You've got this!

1. A Look Within

- How do I see myself in the stories and letters shared in this book?
- What emotions do I experience as I read the letters, and why do I think I feel this way?
- What personal biases or prejudices do I need to confront and overcome?
- How can I foster a spirit of love, light, and laughter in my interactions with others?

2. Fluidity of Innerstanding

- What new perspectives have I gained about the experiences of women from different backgrounds?
- How can I cultivate greater empathy and understanding in my daily interactions?
- In what ways have my own experiences shaped my views about Black women / White women.
- How can I use my personal journey and experiences to contribute to healing and unity among women?

3. Intentional Action

- How can I be an advocate?
- What steps can I take to ensure I do my part to uplift women who look different than me?
- How can I build stronger, more meaningful connections with women of different races and backgrounds?
- What role can I play in creating a more inclusive and supportive community?

REFLECTION & DISCUSSION

Book Club Questions

The *Dear White Woman, Dear Black Woman* book club questions are designed to spark meaningful dialogue, deepen our understanding, and inspire us to take actionable steps towards fostering unity and healing. Let's embrace this opportunity to reflect on our own experiences, challenge our assumptions, and explore how we can contribute to moving humanity forward. As we delve into these questions, let's approach our conversation with openness, empathy, and a willingness to learn from one another.

Feel free to share your thoughts, ask questions, and engage in respectful and thoughtful discussion. Together, we can create a space where every voice is heard and valued.

We can do this. . . we can heal the soul of our nation and world. Women. . . it starts with us. So let's do this, let's have the conversation.

Innerstanding

- What were your initial thoughts and feelings after reading the letters?
- Were there letters or any particular letter that resonated with you the most, and why?
- Did you find your own beliefs or assumptions being challenged?
- In what ways did the book inspire you to reflect on your own experiences with women of different backgrounds and cultures?
- How did the letters help you understand the experiences of women from different backgrounds?

- Share a moment that caused you to better understand a woman different than you yet same?

Intentional Action
- What actions can you take in your own life to promote understanding and unity among women of diverse backgrounds?
- How can the lessons from the book be applied to create positive change and bridge the divide between women?

The Lessons and the Impact
- Was there a quote or passage from the book that stood out to you?
- Was there any particular letter that caused you to look deeper within?
- Why did it stand out and why did it have an impact on you?

Beyond the Pages. . .
- How can this book serve as a starting point for future conversations about racial understanding?
- What are some practical ways we can build bridges between different women in our daily lives?
- How can we create safe spaces for open and honest dialogue?
- What is your commitment after reading *Dear White Woman Dear Black Woman*?

Questions for White Women:
- What assumptions do I hold about race, and how do they impact my actions and decisions?
- Am I listening without judgment when Black women share their experiences of discrimination or injustice?

REFLECTION & DISCUSSION

- What resources, books, or communities can I engage with to better understand my privilege and its impact on others?
- How am I using my platform and influence to amplify Black voices and experiences?
- Am I actively seeking out the perspectives and expertise of Black women in my industry or community?

Questions for Black Women:

- How can I protect my peace and well-being while engaging in difficult conversations about race and equity?
- What assumptions do I hold about White women that no longer serve me well?
- What support would be most helpful from White women in shared spaces?
- What experience have I had when it comes to allyship and support from White women in my personal and professional life? In what ways has the support impacted my life?
- How can I participate in advancing a healthy relationship with White women without feeling the burdened?